Also available from Summertown Texts:

*The Children's Catechism:*
*A New Modern Version*

by Philip Rollinson
and
Mark E. Ross

ISBN: 0-9614303-2-X

A Direct, Simple, Straightforward Review of the Essentials
of the Faith

# The
# Westminster
# Confession of
# Faith

## An Authentic Modern Version

by
Douglas F. Kelly
Hugh W. McClure, III
and
Philip Rollinson

Summertown Texts
Signal Mountain, Tennessee

Summertown Texts
PO Box 453
Signal Mountain, TN 37377-0453
1 (800) 742-5710

Fourth Edition
2004

ISBN: 1-893009-08-4

Printed in the United States of America by Faith Printing Company

# Contents

Preface ........................................................................................ vii

Introduction .................................................................................. ix

The Westminster Confession

1. Holy Scripture ........................................................................ 1
2. God and the Holy Trinity ........................................................ 7
3. God's Eternal Decrees ........................................................... 9
4. Creation ................................................................................. 13
5. Providence ............................................................................. 14
6. The Fall of Man, Sin, and the Punishment for Sin ................ 18
7. God's Covenant with Man ..................................................... 20
8. Christ the Mediator ............................................................... 23
9. Free Will ................................................................................ 27
10. Effectual Calling ................................................................... 29
11. Justification ........................................................................... 31
12. Adoption ............................................................................... 34
13. Sanctification ........................................................................ 35
14. Saving Faith .......................................................................... 37
15. Repentance Leading to Life .................................................. 39
16. Good Works .......................................................................... 41
17. The Perseverance of Christians ........................................... 45
18. The Assurance of Grace and Salvation ................................ 47
19. The Law of God ..................................................................... 50
20. Christian Freedom and Freedom of Conscience .................. 54
21. Religious Worship and the Sabbath Day .............................. 57
22. Lawful Oaths and Vows ........................................................ 62
23. Civil Authorities .................................................................... 64
24. Marriage and Divorce ........................................................... 67
24. Of Marriage and Divorce (UP) .............................................. 69
24. Of Marriage and Divorce (26,PC) ......................................... 70
25. The Church ........................................................................... 73
26. The Fellowship of God's People ........................................... 75
27. The Sacraments .................................................................... 77
28. Baptism ................................................................................. 79
29. The Lord's Supper ................................................................ 81
30. Condemnation by the Church ............................................... 85
31. Synods and Councils ............................................................ 87
32. The Condition of Man after Death and the Resurrection of the Dead .... 89
33. The Last Judgment ............................................................... 91
34. The Holy Spirit ...................................................................... 93
35. The Gospel of the Love of God and Missions ....................... 95

Appendix ..................................................................................... 97

# Preface to the Fourth Edition

This edition brings the history of changes in the American editions of the *Confession* up-to-date and also broadens the focus to include the Cumberland Presbyterian Church (CPC), Orthodox Presbyterian Church (OPC), Presbyterian Church in America (PCA), and Evangelical Presbyterian Church (EPC).

There has also been a change in format involving the presentation of the biblical proof texts. Previous Summertown editions used an elaborate system of parentheses and brackets to indicate which proof texts had been added and which deleted by the Presbyterian Church in the United States of America (PCUSA) in its revision of 1894, and by the Presbyterian Church in the United States (PCUS) in an even more extensive revision in 1910. Since both these bodies were reunited into the Presbyterian Church (U.S.A.) in 1983 and the separate northern and southern churches no longer exist, distinguishing their separate changes to the proof texts seems to be no longer relevant, even in an academic sense. Furthermore, with the union of PCUSA with the United Presbyterian Church of North America (accomplished in 1958, creating UPCUSA), UPCUSA dropped all the proof texts from its next edition of the *Confession,* and PCUSA's new chapter on marriage, done in 1953, has no accompanying proof texts either. Finally, the Presbyterian Church (USA)'s current edition of the *Confession* in its *Book* of *Confessions* (1996) lists only the proof texts as modified by PCUS in 1910.

The Associate Reformed Presbyterian Church (ARP) still lists only the proof texts of the original British edition, as does the current PCA edition (1990); neither church has any of the PCUSA or PCUS modifications. The official paperback edition of the OPC's *Confession* along with the *Larger* and *Shorter Catechisms,* published by Great Commission Publications (1978, fourteenth printing, 2003) has no proof texts at all; neither does their separate edition of the *Confession* alone (eleventh printing, 2001) nor their study edition, *The Westminster Confession of Faith with a parallel Modern English Study Version* (GCO, 1993). Finally, in its latest edition (2002), the Evangelical Presbyterian Church (EPC) simply lists all the proof texts that have ever been adduced to support the positions in the

*Confession,* whether from the original British edition or subsequent American editions. We have treated the proof texts in the same way here in this fourth edition, listing them conveniently after each section of each chapter. We also include use of the General Note added by PCUS in 1910:

> General Note: At several points the Confession of Faith is more specific in its statements than the Scriptures. These statements are inferences drawn from the Scriptures or from statements based on the Scriptures, or from the experience and observation of the Church. In such cases, no texts are cited, but reference is made to this General Note.

# Introduction

This is a study edition of *The Westminster Confession of Faith,* the best known and most famous confessional document coming out of the Protestant Reformation. Many believe it is the greatest single statement of Reformed Christian doctrine, and it remains to this day the standard confessional expression of most Presbyterians around the world. This edition is designed for study groups, Sunday-school classes, officer training, and seminary education, as well as for anyone of any denomination who wants to find out what the *Confession* says, which biblical proof texts are used to support its doctrinal positions, and what changes have been made to its text over the years.

The core of this edition is an accurate rendering into contemporary English of the original *Westminster Confession* as modified by American Presbyterians in 1788. The *Confession* was written between 1643 and 1646, and so, like the English of the King James Bible (1611), has become linguistically obsolete. To be sure, much of it can still be understood by the modern reader, but at the same time, much of it cannot, and some of it has simply become incomprehensible to all but experts in seventeenth-century literature. Since almost all the officers in Presbyterian churches are bound to subscribe to the doctrines articulated in the *Confession,* this modern version makes it possible for them as well as for lay men and women to understand exactly what those doctrinal positions are.

Also included in this edition are all the changes made to the text of the *Confession* by American Presbyterians (with the exceptions of Cumberland Presbyterians and the United Presbyterian Church of North America; see below). The only really substantive changes in the American edition of 1788 concern statements about the relationship of secular government to the church, primarily in Chapters 23 and 31, which reflect the purpose of the Westminster Assembly, called by Parliament in 1643 to create a new state religion to replace the previous state religion, the Anglican Church (now, of course, reinstated, since 1660). Chapters 23 and 31 of the original English edition establish secular authority in and over church affairs. With a constitutional commitment to the clear

# Introduction

separation of church and state, American Presbyterians were unwilling to allow any such secular influence on or control of religion. The great division effected from 1861 to 1865 into the Presbyterian Church in the United States of America (PCUSA) and the Presbyterian Chuirch in the United States (PCUS) did not create any further changes in the text of the *Confession* up to 1902, with one exception—after the Civil War both bodies dropped the final sentence from 24.3 specifically limiting remarriage to a relative of a deceased wife or husband. Otherwise, until then both used fundamentally the same edition except that PCUSA redid the proof texts in 1894.

Early in the twentieth century, both PCUSA in 1903 and PCUS subsequently added two new chapters to the original thirty-three, "Of the Holy Spirit" and "Of the Gospel of the Love of God and Missions" (PCUSA, simply entitled "Of the Gospel" in the identical PCUS version). PCUSA put these two at the end as new chapters 34 and 35; PCUS interpolated them as new chapters 9 and 10 and renumbered the subsequent chapters (with only one verbal alteration, "these" to "those" in 9.4). PCUSA also added at that time a "Declaratory Statement," affirmed by its presbyteries in 1902, elaborating and commenting on the original Chapters 3 and 10. This addition "disavows" what are vaguely referred to as "certain inferences drawn from statements in the Confession of Faith" in Chapters 3 and 10. The Declaration deliberately blurs the clearly predestinarian teaching about election and reprobation in Chapter 3 of the original, and then with reference to section 3 of Chapter 10, assures the reader that all children dying in infancy, not just the elect ones, as the original indicates, will automatically go to heaven. PCUS did not follow suit here, but both churches did independently write new versions of Chapter 24 on marriage in the twentieth century.

Our modern version here is of the basic pre-1900 American edition. Also included are the new Chapters 34 and 35, the "Declaratory Statement," and all three versions of Chapter 24 on marriage. The Appendix, moreover, describes and gives a precise historical collation of all the changes to the original text made by American Presbyterians. Consequently this is a complete study edition.

# Introduction

The life of the *Confession* continues to unfold. First was the precedent set by the Presbyterian Church of England, which in 1890 added to the Confession twenty four "Articles of the Faith" (Schaff, 3:916-919) designed not to replace but to supplement the Westminster standards as a more brief and accessible expression of them. PCUSA followed suit with "A Brief Statement of the Reformed Faith, 1902." In 1925 the United Presbyterian Church of North America (UPCNA) went a step farther with a much longer "Confessional Statement." The Preamble to this new document concludes that "This statement contains the substance of the Wesminster symbols, together with certain present-day convictions of the United Presbyterian Church" (Schaff, 3:925). Although UPCNA still claimed adherance to the Westminster standards, in those cases where the positions of the new Confession differed from the older ones, "its [the new Confession's] declarations are to prevail" (Schaff, 3:924).

Their were further important developments in the largest Presbyterian denomination in America in the last half of the twentieth century. First UPCUSA wrote still another new confession, identified as "The Confession of 1967." Secondly this 1967 standard was used as the capstone of a *Book of Confessions,* which in its final form contained the following ten texts: the Nicene Creed, the Apostle's Creed, the Scots Confession (1560), the Heidelberg Catechism (1563), the Second Helvetic Confession (1566), the Westminster Confession, the Westminster Shorter Catechism, the Westminster Larger Catechism, the Theological Declaration of Barmen (1934), and the new Confession of 1967. Thirdly, to these ten, PC (USA) has added still another "Brief Statement of Faith" as an eleventh and (so far) final text. Although the "Confession of 1967" is not supported by Biblical proof texts, the "Brief Statement" is, along with supporting references to passages in the other, earlier confessions.

There are two significant assumptions underlying this *Book of Confessions.* The first is that every age needs its own confessional statement with its own special focus, i.e., different times require different confessional positions. This is particularly obvious with the inclusion of the Scottish Confession from John Knox's day, because that standard was discarded by Scottish Presbyterians themselves,

## Introduction

who replaced it with the obviously superior *Wesminster Confession* in 1647. And, indeed, this assumption is stated explicitly in the Preface to "The Confession of 1967:" "In every age the church has expressed its witness in words and deeds as the need of the time required" (9.03). The second assumption, also explicitly articulated in the same passage, is that no confessional standard has permanent declarative authority: "No one type of confession is exclusively valid, no one statement is irreformable." Finally, while the presence of the Heidelberg Catechism and Helvetic Confession in the *Book of Confessions* is an inclusive, ecumenical gesture aimed at the Reformed churches in America, whose doctrinal standards are reflected in these two documents (along with a third, the Canons of Dort), the authority of the *Westminster Confession* itself is by the same token diluted and undermined.

The Associate Reformed Presbyterian Church (ARP) adopted a version of the *Confession* in 1799 different from the text adopted by other American Presbyterians in 1788. The ARP version has significantly different readings in Chapters 20, 23, 25, and 31 (see the Appendix). The changes in Chapters 23 and 31 are interesting, because instead of allowing the interference of secular authority into church affairs, as the original has it, the ARP's revision reverses the influence and insists on religious interference in secular affairs. For example, where the original British edition indicates that the civil magistrate shall "call synods, . . . be present at them, and . . . provide that whatsoever is transacted in them is according to the mind of God" (23.3), the ARPs have it that the magistrates "are bound to execute their respective offices in a subserviency thereunto ['the gospel revelation'], administering government on Christian principles, and ruling in the fear of God, according to the directions of his word" and that the civil authorities "are bound to promote the Christian religion, as the most valuable interest of their subjects" (23.3). Instead of changing this position in the twentieth century, the ARPs have simply added a note (among several) at the end of their edition of the *Confession,* which, while refering explicitly to 20.4 (on the extent of Christian liberty), flatly contradicts the ARP version as well as the original content of 23.3:

> In a democratic society, where the Church and the
> State, with regard to their functions and authority, are

# Introduction

entirely separate, this must be interpreted to conform to the principles of separation. Certainly the Church believes in the right of the civil magistrate to punish evildoers, but it does not accept the principle of ecclesiastical subordination to the civil authority, nor does it accept the principle of ecclesiastical authority over the State. (The Standards of the Associate Reformed Presbyterian Church [2000], 71-72).

Among these notes at the end of their edition of the *Confession* is also included the identical comment from PCUSA's "Declaratory Statement" softening the strong position on predestination in Chapter 3 (these notes do not repeat the other part of the "Declaratory Statement" to the effect that all children dying in infancy are saved). In the twentieth century the ARPs also adopted the new American Chapters 34 and 35, but kept the original Chapter 24 on marriage. They have continued to make minor changes to the wording of the *Confession* (the latest to 24.4 in 2001).

Another early American group, the Cumberland Presbyterian Church (CPC), founded in 1810 in western Tennessee, has gone its own way with the Westminster Standards. The Cumberland Presbyterians originally added a "Brief Statement" in 1813 articulating their explicit exceptions to four theological positions in the *Westminster Confession*: (a) double predestination; (b) limited atonement; (c) salvation only for elect children dying in infancy; and (d) irresistable grace. Subsequently the CPC used the *Westminster Confession* as the basis of a revised *Confession* in 1829, which had the specific aim of removing the "hyper-Calvinism" of the original and replacing those passages with different wordings. Major changes were made to chapters 3 (Of God's Eternal Decrees), 9 (Of Free Will), 10 (Of Effectual Calling), 11 (Of Justification), and 17 (Of the Perseverance of the Saints).

Ultimately unsatisfied with the result, since the entire fabric of the *Westminster Confession* is Calvinistic, a further, more drastic revision was completed in 1883, which amounted to a new *Confession*. In 1984, in conjunction with the Second Cumberland Presbyterian Church (now the Cumberland Presbyterian Church in America), CPC adopted an even more extensive "revision." Since even the early changes to the *Westminster Confession* by CPC were aimed at altering its basic Calvinistic character, and since the ultimate 1984 *Confession of Faith* does not even resemble the *Westminster Confession,* we have not included any of the CPC changes in the Appendix to this edition.

Three other Presbyterian bodies should be noted. In the 1930s John Gresham Machen led the formation of a new conservative denomination, the Presbyterian Church of America, which has since changed its name to the Orthodox Presbyterian Church (OPC). The OPCs have adopted the basic pre-1900 American edition of the *Confession,* including the original chapter on marriage, but not the new American Chapters 34 and 35. They have made only three substantive changes to the original text. First is the omission of two sentences. One at the end of 22.3 is about it being sinful to refuse to take an oath demanded on valid grounds by lawful authority (here they have followed the PCUSA revision of 1903; see the Appendix). The second sentence omitted is at the end of 24.4 prohibiting marriage to close relatives of a deceased spouse (also following earlier revisions by PCUSA and PCUS prior to 1903, before these two wrote entirely new chapters on marriage later in the twentieth century). Finally, a very strong anti-Catholic clause at the end of 25.6, indicating that the pope is the antichrist (for the reasoning of the Westminster Assembly here, see Gerstner, et al., *A Guide, The Westminster Confession: Commentary*, 131) has been dropped, but the preceding clause has been retained, which makes the explicit point that the pope is not and cannot be the head of the church.

While the ARP edition also drops this explicit reference to the pope, it does allude to him by adding that "nor can mere man in any sense be the head thereof" (25.6). The edition of the Evangelical Presbyterian Church (EPC) drops any explicit or implicit references to the pope; its 25.6 simply and irenically reads: "There is no other head of the church than the Lord Jesus Christ." Earlier PCUSA and PCUS editions of the *Confession* drop any explicit reference to the pope at all (with one exception at the end of 23.4, where it is explained that the pope has no legitimate claim to secular authority or judicial powers; the EPC edition also retains this passage). The OPC edition additionally lets stand a strongly anti-Catholic sentiment, forbidding Christians from marrying "infidels, papists, or other idolaters" (24.3), as did PCUSA and PCUS, until each dropped the original chapter in its entirety in favor of completely new chapters. About forty years later, a similarly conservative church, the Presbyterian Church in America (PCA), which grew mainly out of PCUS in 1973, adopted essentially the same version of the *Confession* as the OPCs earlier. In addition to removing the explicit reference to the pope in 25.6, the ARPs have also removed the reference to "papists" in 24.3.

Of course, where there are sharp differences between Presbyterian and Roman Catholic doctrine, these are always duly noted in the original *Confession* and in all the American editions as well. In Chapter 29 on "The Lord's Supper," for example, 29.2 explicitly attacks the Roman Catholic mass (slightly softened by PCUSA and PCUS) and follows in 29.4 with indirect attacks on private masses, denying the cup to the congregation, and elevation of the host (all practices of the Roman Catholic Church). Then, 29.6 attacks the doctrine of transubstantiation.

The Evangelical Presbyterian Church (EPC), formed in 1981 before the reunion of PCUS and UPCUSA in 1983, is the newest of the Presbyterian bodies. The EPCs have gone in exactly the opposite direction from the OPC and PCA churches in what is certainly the most dramatic new development in the history of the *Confession.* Although the OPC has brought out its own study edition of the *Confession,* which includes a (very conservative) modern language version on the right-hand page facing the text of the original on the left (Great Commission Publications, 1993), the Preface to this edition makes the emphatic point that the modernization is in no sense a substitute for the original: "it [the Modern English Study Version] is not intended to take the place of the Church's Confession as the authoritative subordinate doctrinal standard of the Church any more than the modern English versions of the Holy Scriptures are intended to take the place of the Scriptures in the original languages" (4). The analogy drawn here between the original English wording of the *Confession* and the original Hebrew and Greek wording of the Bible is surely not meant to imply that the Westminster standards are endowed with some divinely sanctioned status that renders them above and superior to other theological and confessional statements, even in their very wording.

# Introduction

Whatever the case, rather than attempting to perpetuate the original words of the *Confession* in this way, the EPC has dropped the original wording altogether in favor of a modern language version that perpetuates the original meaning by making it completely understandable to the contemporary reader. So, the EPCs have adopted a tailor-made version of the Summertown modernization as their official, doctrinal standard. This specialized EPC edition also includes the PCUS chapter (24) on marriage as well as the new American chapters on the Holy Spirit and the gospel (34 and 35). It does not include the "Declaratory Statement" from PCUSA.

# The
# Westminster
# Confession of
# Faith

# Chapter 1
## Holy Scripture

1. Our natural understanding and the works of creation and providence so clearly show God's goodness, wisdom, and power that human beings have no excuse.[1] However, these means alone cannot provide that knowledge of God and of his will which is necessary for salvation.[2] Therefore it pleased the Lord at different times and in various ways to reveal himself and to declare that this revelation contains his will for his church.[3] Afterwards it pleased God to put this entire revelation into writing so that the truth might be better preserved and transmitted and that the church, confronted with the corruption of the flesh and the evil purposes of Satan and the world, might be more securely established and comforted.[4] Since God no longer reveals himself to his people in those earlier ways,[5] Holy Scripture is absolutely essential.[6]

1. Rom 2.14-15, 1.19-20, Ps 19.1-4, Rom 1.32, 2.1.
2. 1 Cor 1.21, 2.13-14, 2.9-12, Acts 4.12, Rom 10.13-14.
3. Heb 1.1-2, Gal 1.11-12, Dt 4.12-14.
4. Prv 22.19-21, Lk 1.3-4, Rom 15.4, Mt 4.4,7,10, Is 8.19-20,
   Lk 24.27, 2 Tm 3.16, 2 Pt 3.15-16.
5. Heb 1.1-2, see General Note.
6. 2 Tm 3.15-16, 2 Pt 1.10, Lk 16.29-31, Heb 2.1-3.

## Holy Scripture

2. What we call Holy Scripture or the written word of God now includes all the books of the Old and the New Testament which are:

The Old Testament:

| | | |
|---|---|---|
| Genesis | 2 Chronicles | Daniel |
| Exodus | Ezra | Hosea |
| Leviticus | Nehemiah | Joel |
| Numbers | Esther | Amos |
| Deuteronomy | Job | Obadiah |
| Joshua | Psalms | Jonah |
| Judges | Proverbs | Micah |
| Ruth | Ecclesiastes | Nahum |
| 1 Samuel | Song of Solomon | Habakkuk |
| 2 Samuel | Isaiah | Zephaniah |
| 1 Kings | Jeremiah | Haggai |
| 2 Kings | Lamentations | Zechariah |
| 1 Chronicles | Ezekiel | Malachi |

The New Testament:

| | | |
|---|---|---|
| Matthew | Ephesians | Hebrews |
| Mark | Philippians | James |
| Luke | Colossians | 1 Peter |
| John | 1 Thessalonians | 2 Peter |
| Acts | 2 Thessalonians | 1 John |
| Romans | 1 Timothy | 2 John |
| 1 Corinthians | 2 Timothy | 3 John |
| 2 Corinthians | Titus | Jude |
| Galatians | Philemon | Revelation |

All of these books are inspired by God and are the rule of faith and life. [7]

7. Lk 16.29,31, Eph 2.20, Rv 22.18-19, 2 Tm 3.16, Mt 11.27.

3. The books usually called the Apocrypha are not divinely inspired and are not part of the canon of Scripture. They therefore have no authority in the church of God and are not to be valued or used as anything other than human writings.[8]

> 8. Lk 24.27,44, Rom 3.2, 2 Pt 1.21. The Canon of Scripture is not established by explicit passages, but by the testimony of Jesus and his apostles; of ancient manuscripts and versions; of ancient Christian writers and church councils, and by the internal evidence exhibited in the separate books.

4. The Bible speaks authoritatively and so deserves to be believed and obeyed. This authority does not depend on the testimony of any man or church but completely on God, its author, who is himself truth. The Bible therefore is to be accepted as true, because it is the word of God.[9]

> 9. 2 Pt 1.19,21, 2 Tm 3.16, 1 Jn 5.9, 1 Thes 2.13, Gal 1.11-12.

5. We may be influenced by the testimony of the church to value the Bible highly and reverently, and Scripture itself shows in so many ways that it is God's word; for example, in its spiritual subject matter, in the effectiveness of its teaching, the majesty of its style, the agreement of all its parts, its unified aim from beginning to end (to give all glory to God), the full revelation it makes of the only way of man's salvation, its many other incomparably outstanding features, and its complete perfection. However, we are completely persuaded and assured of the infallible truth and divine authority of the Bible only by the inward working of the Holy Spirit, who testifies by and with the word in our hearts.[10]

> 10. 1 Tm 3.15, 1 Jn 2.20,27, Jn 16.13-14, 1 Cor 2.10-12, Is 59.21, 1 Cor 2.6-9.

## Holy Scripture

6. The whole purpose of God about everything pertaining to his own glory and to man's salvation, faith, and life is either explicitly stated in the Bible or may be deduced as inevitably and logically following from it.[11] Nothing is at any time to be added to the Bible, either from new revelations of the Spirit or from traditions of men.[12] Nevertheless we do recognize that the inward illumination of the Spirit of God is necessary for a saving understanding of the things which are revealed in the word.[13] We also recognize that some provisions for the worship of God and the government of the church are similar to secular activities and organizations; these are to be directed according to our natural understanding and our Christian discretion and should conform to the general rules of the word, which are always to be observed.[14]

11. Mk 7.5-7.
12. 2 Tm 3.15-17, Gal 1.8-9, 2 Thes 2.2. This statement is an inference from the sufficiency of the Scriptures.
13. Jn 6.45, 1 Cor 2.9-10,12.
14. 1 Cor 11.13-14, 14.26,40.

7. The meanings of all the passages in the Bible are not equally obvious, nor is any individual passage equally clear to everyone.[15] However, everything which we have to know, believe, and observe in order to be saved is so clearly presented and revealed somewhere in the Bible that the uneducated as well as the educated can sufficiently understand it by the proper use of the ordinary means of grace.[16]

15. 2 Pt 3.16, Jn 6.60, 16.17.
16. Ps 119.105,130, Acts 17.11-12.

4

8. The Old Testament in Hebrew (the native language of the ancient people of God) and the New Testament in Greek (the language most widely known internationally at the time the New Testament was written) were directly inspired by God[17] and have been kept uncontaminated throughout time by his special care and providence. They are therefore authentic and are to be the church's ultimate source of appeal in every religious controversy.[18] The original languages of the Bible, however, are not understood by all of God's people. But all of God's people have a right to and interest in the Bible, and God himself commands them to read it thoroughly with awe and reverence for him.[19] Consequently the Bible should be translated into the native language of every people to whom it is introduced. Then, the word of God will live fully in everyone; everyone will be able to worship God in an acceptable way; and all believers may have hope through the endurance and the encouragement of the Bible.[20]

> 17. See note under Section 3 above.
> 18. Mt 5.18, Is 8.20, Acts 15.14-18, Jn 5.9,46.
> 19. Jn 5.39, 2 Tm 3.14-15, 2 Pt 1.19, Acts 17.11.
> 20. 1 Cor 14.6,9,11-12,24,27-28, Col 3.16, Rom 15.4, Mt 28.19-20.

9. The infallible standard for the interpretation of the Bible is the Bible itself. And so any question about the true and complete sense of a passage in the Bible (which is a unified whole) can be answered by referring to other passages which speak more clearly.[21]

> 21. 2 Pt 1.20-21, Acts 15.15, Jn 5.46, Mt 4.5-7, 12.1-7.

10. The Holy Spirit speaking in the Bible is the supreme judge of all religious controversies, all decisions of religious councils, all the opinions of ancient writers, all human teachings, and every private opinion.[22] We are to be satisfied with the judgment of him who is and can be the only judge.

> 22. Mt 22.29,31, Eph 2.20, Acts 28.25, Lk 10.26,
> Gal 1.10, 1 Jn 4.1-6.

# Chapter 2
## God and the Holy Trinity

1. There is only one living and true God,[1] who is infinite in being and perfection,[2] a completely pure spirit,[3] invisible,[4] without parts or emotions,[5] unchangeable,[6] immensely vast,[7] eternal,[8] beyond our full understanding,[9] almighty,[10] completely wise,[11] completely holy,[12] completely free,[13] and completely absolute.[14] He works everything according to the purpose of his own unchangeable and completely righteous will[15] for his own glory.[16] He is completely loving,[17] gracious, merciful, and long-suffering. He overflows with goodness and truth. He forgives wickedness, transgression, and sin,[18] and rewards those who diligently seek him.[19] His judgments are completely just and awesome;[20] he hates all sin[21] and will not acquit the guilty.[22]

1. Dt 6.4, 1 Cor 8.4,6, 1 Thes 1.9, Jer 10.10
2. Jb 11.7-9, 26.14, Jer 23.24, Ps 147.5, 1 Kgs 8.27, Ps 139.
3. Jn 4.24.
4. 1 Tm 1.17.
5. Dt 4.15-16, Jn 4.24, Lk 24.39, Acts 14.11,15.
6. Jas 1.17, Mal 3.6.
7. 1 Kgs 8.27, Jer 23.23-24.
8. Ps 90.2, 1 Tm 1.17.
9. Ps 145.3, Rom 11.33.
10. Gn 17.1, Rv 4.8.
11. Rom 16.27.
12. Is 6.3, Rv 4.8.
13. Ps 115.3.
14. Ex 3.14, Is 44.6, Acts 17.24-25.
15. Eph 1.11.
16. Prv 16.4, Rom 11.36, Rv 4.11.
17. 1 Jn 4.8-10,16, Jn 3.16.
18. Ex 34.6-7.
19. Heb 11.6.
20. Neh 9.32-33, Heb 10.28-31.
21. Ps 5.5-6, Hb 1.13.
22. Na 1.2-3, Ex 34.7.

## *God and the Holy Trinity*

2. God has all life, glory, goodness, and blessedness in and of himself.[23] He alone is all-sufficient in and unto himself, nor does he need any of his creations or derive any glory from them. Rather, he manifests his own glory in, by, unto, and on them.[24] He is the only source of all being, by whom, through whom, and to whom everything exists.[25] He has completely sovereign dominion over all things and does with, to, or for them whatever he pleases.[26] Everything is revealed and completely open to him.[27] His knowledge is infinite, infallible, and does not depend on any created being,[28] so that to him nothing is conditional or uncertain.[29] He is completely holy in all his purposes, works, and commands.[30] To him is due whatever worship, service, or obedience he is pleased to require from angels, human beings, and all other creatures.[31]

> 23. Jn 5.26, Acts 7.2, Ps 119.68, 1 Tm 6.15, Rom 9.5.
> 24. Acts 17.24-25, Jb 22.2,23, Ps 50.12, Is 4.12-17.
> 25. Rom 11.36, Is 40.12-17.
> 26. Rv 4.11, 1 Tm 6.15, Dn 4.25, 35, Eph 1.11.
> 27. Heb 4.13.
> 28. Rom 11.33-34, Ps 147.5.
> 29. Acts 15.18, Ez 11.5, Is 46.9-11, Prv 15.3.
> 30. Ps 145.17, Rom 7.12.
> 31. Rv 5.12-14, 7.11-12.

3. In the unity of the Godhead there are three persons, having one substance, power, and eternity: God the Father, God the Son, and God the Holy Spirit.[32] The Father exists. He is not generated and does not come from any source. The Son is eternally generated from the Father,[33] and the Holy Spirit eternally comes from the Father and the Son.[34]

> 32. 1 Jn 5.7, Mt 3.16-17, 28.19, 2 Cor 13.14, Eph 2.18.
> 33. Jn 1.14,18, 17.24, Heb 1.2-6, Col 1.15-17.
> 34. Jn 15.26, Gal 4.6.

# Chapter 3
## God's Eternal Decrees

1. From all eternity and by the completely wise and holy purpose of his own will, God has freely and unchangeably ordained whatever happens.[1] This ordainment does not mean, however, that God is the author of sin (he is not),[2] that he represses the will of his created beings, or that he takes away the freedom or contingency of secondary causes. Rather, the will of created beings and the freedom and contingency of secondary causes are established by him.[3]

    1. Eph 1.11, Rom 11.33, Heb 6.17, Rom 9.15,18, Acts 4.27-28, Mt 10.29-30, Eph 2.10, Is 45.6-7.
    2. Jas 1.13-14,17, 1 Jn 1.5, Eccl 7.29, Ps 5.4.
    3. Acts 2.23, Mt 17.12, Acts 4.27-28, Jn 19.11, Prv 16.33, Acts 27.23-24,34,44.

2. Although God knows whatever may or can happen under all possible circumstances,[4] he has not ordered anything because he foresaw it in the future as something which would happen under such circumstances.[5]

    4. Acts 15.18, 1 Sm 23.11-12, Mt 11.21,23, Ps 139.1-4, Prv 16.33.
    5. Rom 9.11,13,15-16,18, 2 Tm 1.9, Eph 1.4-5.

3. In order to manifest his glory God has ordered that some men and angels be predestined to everlasting life[6] and that others should be foreordained to everlasting death.[7]

    6. 1 Tm 5.21, Mt 25.31,41, Acts 13.48, Rom 8.29-30, Jn 10.27-29, Mk 8.38, Jude 6.
    7. Rom 9.22-23, Eph 1.5-6, Prv 16.4, Mt 25.41, Jude 4.

4. This predestination and foreordination of angels and men are precise and unchangeable. The number and identity of angels and men in each group are certain, definite, and unalterable.[8]

> 8. 2 Tm 2.19, Jn 13.18, 10.14-16,27-29, 6.37-39, Acts 13.48, Jn 17.2,6,9-12.

5. Before the creation of the world,[9] according to his eternal, unchangeable plan[10] and the hidden purpose and good pleasure of his will,[11] God has chosen in Christ[12] those of mankind who are predestined to life and to everlasting glory.[13] He has done this solely out of his own mercy and love and completely to the praise of his wonderful grace.[14] This choice was completely independent of his foresight of how his created beings would be or act. Neither their faith nor good works nor perseverance had any part in influencing his selection.[15]

> 9. Eph 1.4.
> 10. Eph 1.11.
> 11. Eph 1.9.
> 12. 2 Tm 1.9.
> 13. Rom 8.30, 1 Thes 5.9, 1 Pt 5.10.
> 14. Eph 1.5-6,12.
> 15. Rom 9.11,13,15-16, Eph 1.4,6,9, 2 Tm 1.9, Eph 2.8-9.

6. Just as God has determined that the elect shall be glorified, so, too, in the eternal and completely free purpose of his will he has foreordained all the means by which that election is accomplished.[16] And so, those who are chosen, having fallen in Adam, are redeemed by Christ.[17] They are effectually called to faith in Christ by his Spirit working in them at the right time,[18] and they are justified,[19] adopted,[20] sanctified,[21] and kept by his power through faith unto salvation.[22] Only the elect, and no others, are redeemed by Christ, effectually called, justified, adopted, sanctified, and saved.[23]

   16. 1 Pt 1.2, Eph 1.4-5, 2.10, 2 Thes 2.13.
   17. 1 Thes 5.9-10, Ti 2.14, Rom 5.19.
   18. Rom 9.11, 2 Thes 2.13-14, 1 Cor 1.9.
   19. Rom 8.30.
   20. Eph 1.5.
   21. 2 Thes 2.13, Eph 1.4, 1 Thes 4.3.
   22. 1 Pt 1.5, Jn 10.28.
   23. Jn 17.9, Rom 8.28-39, Jn 6.64-65, 8.47, 10.26, 1 Jn 2.19, Acts 13.48.

7. According to the hidden purpose of his own will, by which he offers or withholds mercy at his pleasure, and for the glory of his sovereign power over his creatures, it pleased God to leave the rest of mankind as they are[24] and to ordain them to dishonor and wrath for their sin[25] to the praise of his glorious justice.[26]

   24. Mt 11.25-26, 1 Pt 2.8.
   25. Rom 9.14-22, Jude 4, Rom 2.8-9, 2 Thes 2.10-12.
   26. 2 Tm 2.19-20, Rv 15.3-4.

## God's Eternal Decrees

8. This important and mysterious doctrine of predestination must be treated with special discretion and care, so that, paying attention to and obeying the will of God revealed in his word, human beings may be assured that they have been eternally chosen from the certainty of their effectual calling. In this way the doctrine of predestination will elicit not only our praise, reverence, and admiration for God, but also a humble and diligent life, fully supporting everyone who sincerely obeys the gospel.[27]

27. Rom 9.20, 11.33, Dt 29.29, 2 Pt 1.10, Eph 1.6, Rom 11.5-6,20, 8.33, Lk 10.20, see General Note.

# Chapter 4
## Creation

1. In the beginning it pleased God the Father, Son, and Holy Spirit [1] to create the world out of nothing in order to reveal the glory of his eternal power, wisdom, and goodness.[2] He made everything in the world, visible and invisible, in the space of six days, and it was very good.[3]

   1. Heb 1.2, Jn 1.2-3, Gn 1.1-3, Jb 26.13, 33.4, Rom 11.36, 1 Cor 8.6.
   2. Rom 1.20, Jer 10.12, Ps 104.24, 33.5-6.
   3. Gn 1, Heb 11.3, Col 1.16, Acts 17.24, Ex 20.11.

2. After God had made all the other creatures, he created human beings, male and female,[4] with reasoning, immortal souls.[5] He endowed them with knowledge, righteousness, and true holiness in his own image[6] and wrote his law in their hearts.[7] God also gave them the ability to obey his law and the potential to disobey it; i.e., he gave them freedom of their own wills, which could change.[8] In addition to this law written in their hearts, they were commanded not to eat from the Tree of the Knowledge of Good and Evil.[9] As long as they obeyed God's law and kept this commandment, they were happy in fellowship with God[10] and had dominion over the other creatures.[11]

   4. Gn 1.27.
   5. Gn 2.7, Eccl 12.7, Lk 23.43, Mt 10.28, Ps 8.5-6, Gn 2.19-20.
   6. Gn 1.26, Col 3.10, Eph 4.24.
   7. Rom 2.14-15.
   8. Eccl 7.29, Gn 3.6,17, 2.16-17, Col 3.10, Eph 4.24.
   9. Gn 2.16-17.
   10. Gn 2.17, 3.8-11,23.
   11. Gn 1.26,28, Ps 8.6-8, Gn 1.29-30.

# Chapter 5
## Providence

1. God, who created everything, also upholds everything. He directs, regulates, and governs every creature, action, and thing, from the greatest to the least,[1] by his completely wise and holy providence.[2] He does so in accordance with his infallible foreknowledge[3] and the voluntary, unchangeable purpose of his own will,[4] all to the praise of the glory of his wisdom, power, justice, goodness, and mercy.[5]

   1. Heb 1.3, Dn 4.34-35, Ps 135.6, Acts 17.25-26,28, Jb 38-41, Mt 10.29-31, 6.26,30, Neh 9.6, Ps 114.14-16.
   2. Prv 15.3, 2 Chr 16.9, Ps 104.24, Ps 145.17.
   3. Acts 15.18, Ps 94.8-11.
   4. Eph 1.11, Ps 33.10-11.
   5. Is 63.14, Eph 3.10, Rom 9.17, Gn 45.7, Ps 145.7.

2. God is the first cause, and in relationship to him everything happens unchangeably and infallibly.[6] However, by this same providence, he orders things to happen from secondary causes. As a result of these secondary causes, some things must inevitably happen;[7] others may or may not happen depending on the voluntary intentions of the agents involved; and some things do not have to happen but may, depending on other conditions.[8]

   6. Acts 2.23, see under figures 3 and 4 above, Jer 32.19.
   7. Gn 8.22, Jer 31.35.
   8. Ex 21.13, Dt 19.5, 1 Kgs 22.28,34, Is 10.6-7, Gn 50.19-20.

# *Providence*

3. God uses ordinary means to work out his providence day by day.[9] But, as he pleases,[10] he may work without,[11] beyond,[12] or contrary to these means.

> 9. Acts 27.24,31,44, Is 55.10-11, Hos 2.21-22.
> 10. 2 Kgs 6.6, Dn 3.27, 1 Kgs 18.17-39, Jn 11.43-45, Rom 1.4.
> 11. Hos 1.7, Mt 4.4, Jb 34.10.
> 12. Rom 4.19-21.

4. God's providence reveals his almighty power, unknowable wisdom, and infinite goodness. His providence extends even to the fall[13] and to all other sins of angels and men.[14] These sins are not simply allowed by God, but are bound,[15] ordered, and governed by him in the fulness of his wisdom and power so that they fulfill his own holy purposes.[16] However, the sinfulness still belongs to the creature and does not proceed from God, whose holy righteousness does not and cannot cause or approve sin.[17]

> 13. This statement is sustained by the doctrines of God's decrees and providence. See citations under Chapter 3 and Chapter 5, Sections 1,2,3.
> 14. Rom 11.32-34, 2 Sm 24.1, 1 Chr 21.1, 1 Kgs 22.22-23, 1 Chr 10.4,13-14, 2 Sm 16.10, Acts 2.23, 4.27-28, see citations under Chapter 3 and Chapter 5, Sections 1,2,3, Is 45.7.
> 15. Acts 14.16, Ps 76.10, 2 Kgs 19.28, Is 10.5-7,12,15.
> 16. Gn 50.20, Is 10.6-7,12-15, see under figure 15 above.
> 17. Jas 1.13-14,17, 1 Jn 2.16, Ps 50.21.

5. In the fulness of his wisdom, righteousness, and grace God often allows his own children to be tempted in various ways and for a time to pursue the corruption of their own hearts. God does this to chastise them for their previous sins and to reveal to them the hidden strength of corruption and deceitfulness in their hearts, so that they may be humbled.[18] In addition to various other just and holy results, believers are thereby raised to a closer and more constant dependence on God for their support and are also made more alert in detecting and resisting opportunities to sin.[19]

18. 2 Chr 32.25,26,31, 2 Sm 24.1,25, Dt 8.2, Lk 22.31-32.
19. 2 Cor 12.7-9, Ps 73, 77.1-12, Mk 14.66-72, Jn 21.15-19.

6. It is different for the wicked and the ungodly. As punishment for their previous sins, God, the righteous judge, spiritually blinds and hardens them in their own sinfulness.[20] From them God not only withdraws his grace, by which they might have been spiritually enlightened,[21] but sometimes he also withdraws whatever gift of spiritual understanding they already had[22] and deliberately exposes them to the opportunities for sinning which their corrupt natures naturally seek.[23] He thereby gives them over to their own desires, to the temptations of the world, and to the power of Satan,[24] and so it happens that they harden themselves even under those circumstances which God uses to soften others.[25]

20. Rom 1.24-26,28, 11.7-8, 2 Thes 2.11-12.
21. Dt 29.4, Mk 4.11-12.
22. Mt 13.12, 25.29, Acts 13.10-11, 2 Cor 11.13,15.
23. Dt 2.30, 2 Kgs 8.12-13.
24. Ps 81.11-12, 2 Thes 2.10-12, 2 Cor 2.11, 11.3.
25. Ex 7.3, 8.15,32, 2 Cor 2.15-16, Is 8.14, 1 Pt 2.7-8, Is 6.9-10, Acts 28.26-27

## Providence

7. Just as the providence of God in general extends to every creature, so, in a very special way it takes care of his church and orders all things for her good.[26]

> 26. 1 Tm 4.10, Am 9.8-9, Rom 8.28, Is 43.3-5,14, Eph 1.22, Mt 16.18.

# Chapter 6
## The Fall of Man, Sin, and the Punishment for Sin

1. Our first parents were led astray by the cunning temptation of Satan and sinned in eating the forbidden fruit.[1] It pleased God to allow them to sin, because in his wisdom and holiness he planned to order their sin to his own glory.[2]

   > 1. Gn 3.13, 2 Cor 11.3, Gn 3.1-14.
   > 2. Rom 11.32, 5.19-21.

2. By this sin they fell from their original righteousness and fellowship with God,[3] and so became dead in sin[4] and completely polluted in all their faculties and parts of body and soul.[5]

   > 3. Gn 3.6-8, Eccl 7.29, Rom 3.23, Gn 2.17.
   > 4. Gn 2.17, Eph 2.1-3, Rom 5.12,
   > 5. Ti 1.15, Gn 6.5, Jer 17.9, Rom 3.10-19, 8.6-8, Ps 58.1-5.

3. Since Adam and Eve are the root of all mankind, the guilt for this sin has been imputed to all human beings,[6] who are their natural descendants and have inherited the same death in sin and the same corrupt nature.[7]

   > 6. Gn 1.27-28, 2.16-17, Rom 5.12,15-19, Acts 17.26, 1 Cor 15.21-22,45,49.
   > 7. Ps 51.5, Gn 5.3, Jb 14.4, 15.14, Jn 3 and 6, Rom 3.10-18.

4. This original corruption completely disinclines, incapacitates, and turns us away from every good, while it completely inclines us to every evil.[8] From it proceed all actual sins.[9]

>   8. Rom 5.6, 7.18, 8.7, Col 1.21, Jn 3.6, Gn 6.5, 8.21, Rom 3.10-19.
>   9. Jas 1.14-15, Eph 2.2-3, Mt 15.19.

5. During life on earth this corrupt nature remains in those who are regenerated,[10] and, although it is pardoned and deadened in Christ, yet it and all its impulses are truly and properly sinful.[11]

>   10. 1 Jn 1.8,10, Rom 7.14,17-18,21-23, Jas 3.2, Prv 20.9, Eccl 7.20.
>   11. Rom 7.5,7-8,25, Gal 5.17.

6. Every sin, both original and actual, transgresses the righteous law of God and brings guilt on the sinner.[12] Every sinner is consequently subjected to the wrath of God,[13] the curse of the law,[14] and death,[15] with all the resultant miseries, spiritual, temporal, and eternal.[16]

>   12. 1 Jn 3.4, Rom 2.15, 3.9,19.
>   13. Eph 2.3, Rom 5.12.
>   14. Gal 3.10.
>   15. Rom 6.23, Gn 2.17.
>   16. Eph 4.18, Rom 8.20, Lam 3.39, Mt 25.41, 2 Thes 1.9, Rom 1.21-28, Lv 26.14ff, Dt 28.15ff.

# Chapter 7
## God's Covenant with Man

1. The distance between God and his creation is so great, that, although reasoning creatures owe him obedience as their creator, they nonetheless could never realize any blessedness or reward from him without his willingly condescending to them. And so it pleased God to provide for man by means of covenants.[1]

   1. Is 40.13-17, Jb 9.32-33, 1 Sm 2.25,
      Ps 100.2-3, 113.5-6, Jb 22.2-3, 35.7-8, Lk 17.10,
      Acts 17.24-25, see General Note.

2. The first covenant made with man was a covenant of works.[2] In it life was promised to Adam and through him to his descendants,[3] on the condition of perfect, personal obedience.[4]

   2. Hos 6.7, Gn 2.16-17, Gal 3.10, Rom 5.12,19,
      1 Cor 15.22,47, Gal 3.12.
   3. Rom 5.12-20, 10.5.
   4. Gn 2.17, Gal 3.10; compare Gn 2.16-17 with
      Rom 5.12-14, 10.5, Lk 10.25-28, and with the
      covenants made with Noah and Abraham.

3. By his fall, man made himself incapable of life under that covenant, and so the Lord made a second, the covenant of grace.[5] In it he freely offers sinners life and salvation through Jesus Christ. In order to be saved he requires faith in Jesus[6] and promises to give his Holy Spirit to all who are ordained to life so that they may be willing and able to believe.[7]

   5. Gal 3.21, Rom 3.20-21, 8.3, Gn 3.15, Is 42.6,
      Mt 26.28, Heb 10.5-10.
   6. Mk 16.15-16, Jn 3.16, Rom 10.6,9, Gal 3.11,
      Acts 16.30-31, Mt 28.18-20, Rom 1.16-17.
   7. Ez 36.26-27, Jn 6.37,44-45, 5.37, 3.5-8, Acts 13.48,
      Lk 11.13, Gal 3.14.

4. This covenant of grace is frequently identified in Scripture as a testament, in reference to the death of Jesus Christ, the testator, and to the everlasting inheritance and everything included in that legacy.[8]

> 8. Heb 9.15-17, 7.22, Lk 22.20, 1 Cor 11.25.

5. This covenant was administered differently in the time of the law and in the time of the gospel.[9] Under the law it was administered by promises, prophecies, sacrifices, circumcision, the paschal lamb, and other types and ordinances given to the Jewish people, all foreshadowing Christ.[10] For that time the covenant administered under the law through the operation of the Spirit was sufficient and effective in instructing the elect and building up their faith in the promised Messiah,[11] by whom they had full remission of their sins and eternal salvation. This administration is called the Old Testament.[12]

> 9. 2 Cor 3.6-9, Heb 1.1-2.
> 10. Heb 8-10, Rom 4.11, Col 2.11-12, 1 Cor 5.7, Col 2.17.
> 11. 1 Cor 10.1-4, Heb 11.13, Jn 8.56, Gal 3.6-8.
> 12. Gal 3.7-9,14, Acts 15.11, Rom 3.30.

6. Under the gospel Christ himself, the substance[13] of God's grace, was revealed. The ordinances of this New Testament are the preaching of the word and the administration of the sacraments of baptism and the Lord's supper.[14] Although these are fewer in number and are administered with more simplicity and less outward glory, yet they are available to all nations, Jews and Gentiles,[15] and in them the spiritual power of the covenant of grace is more fully developed.[16] There are not then two essentially different covenants of grace, but one and the same covenant under different dispensations.[17]

13. Gal 2.17, Col 2.17.
14. Mt 28.19-20, 1 Cor 11.23-25, 2 Cor 3.7-11.
15. Mt 28.19, Eph 2.15-19, see under figure 11 above, Lk 2.32, Acts 10.34-35.
16. Heb 12.22-28, Jer 31.33-34, Heb 8.6-13, 2 Cor 3.9-11.
17. Lk 22.20, Heb 8.7-9, Gal 3.14,16, Acts 15.11, Rom 3.21-23,30, Ps 32.1, Rom 4.3,6,16-17,23-24, Heb 13.8, Gal 3.17,29, see context and citations under figure 10 above, Heb 1.1-2.

# Chapter 8
## Christ the Mediator

1. In his eternal purpose it pleased God to choose and ordain the Lord Jesus, his only begotten Son, to be the mediator between God and man.[1] Jesus is the prophet,[2] priest,[3] and king,[4] the head and savior of his church,[5] the heir of all things,[6] and judge of the world.[7] From all eternity God gave him a people to be his seed[8] and to be in time redeemed, called, justified, sanctified, and glorified by him.[9]

   1. Is 42.1, 1 Pt 1.19-20, Jn 3.16, 1 Tm 2.5.
   2. Acts 3.20-22, Dt 18.15.
   3. Heb 5.5-6.
   4. Ps 2.6, Lk 1.33, Is 9.6-7.
   5. Eph 5.23.
   6. Heb 1.2.
   7. Acts 17.31, 2 Cor 5.10.
   8. Jn 17.6, Ps 22.30, Is 53.10, Eph 1.4, Jn 6.37,39.
   9. 1 Tm 2.5-6, Is 55.4-5, 1 Cor 1.30, Mk 10.45, Rom 8.30.

2. The Son of God, the second person of the Trinity, is truly the eternal God, of one substance and equal with the Father. In the fulness of time he took on himself the nature of man,[10] with all the essential qualities and ordinary frailties of man—except that he was sinless.[11] Jesus was conceived by the power of the Holy Spirit in the womb of the Virgin Mary out of her substance.[12] These two complete, perfect, and distinct natures, the Godhead and the manhood, were inseparably joined together in the one person of Jesus without being altered, disunited or mixed together.[13] The person Jesus is truly God and truly man, yet one Christ, the only mediator between God and man.[14]

   10. Jn 1.1,14, 1 Jn 5.20, Phil 2.6, Gal 4.4, Heb 2.14.
   11. Heb 2.14,16-17, 4.15.
   12. Lk 1.27,31,35, Gal 4.4, see under figure 10 above.
   13. Lk 1.35, Col 2.9, Rom 9.5, 1 Pt 3.18, 1 Tm 3.16,
       Mt 16.16, see under figure 12 above.
   14. Rom 1.3-4, 1 Tm 2.5.

3. His human nature being thus united to the divine, the Lord Jesus was sanctified and anointed with the Holy Spirit beyond all measure.[15] He had in him all the treasures of wisdom and knowledge,[16] and in him it pleased the Father that all fulness should dwell.[17] God's purpose was that Jesus, being holy, harmless, undefiled, and full of grace and truth, should be completely equipped to execute the office of mediator and guarantor.[18] Jesus did not take this office himself but was called to it by his Father,[19] who gave and commanded him to use all power and judgment.[20]

   15. Ps 45.7, Jn 3.34, Lk 4.18-19,21, Acts 10.38, Heb 1.8-9.
   16. Col 2.3.
   17. Col 1.19.
   18. Heb 7.26, Jn 1.14, Acts 10.38, Heb 12.24, 7.22,
       Lk 4.18-21.
   19. Heb 5.4-5.
   20. Jn 5.22,27, Mt 28.18, Acts 2.36.

4. The Lord Jesus undertook this office completely voluntarily.[21] In order to discharge it, he was made under[22] and perfectly fulfilled the law.[23] He endured extremely severe torment in his soul[24] and extremely painful suffering in his body.[25] He was crucified and died.[26] He was buried and remained under the power of death, but his body did not decay.[27] On the third day he arose from the dead[28] with the same body in which he had suffered[29] and with which he also ascended into heaven. There he sits at the right hand of his Father,[30] interceding for believers.[31] He will return to judge men and angels at the end of the world.[32]

21. Ps 40.7-8, Heb 10.5-10, Jn 10.18, Phil 2.5-8, Jn 4.34.
22. Gal 4.4.
23. Mt 3.15, 5.17, Jn 17.4.
24. Mt 26.37-38, Lk 22.44, Mt 27.46.
25. Mt 26 and 27.
26. Phil 2.8.
27. Acts 2.23-24,27, Acts 13.37, Rom 6.9, Mt 27.60.
28. 1 Cor 15.3-4.
29. Jn 20.25,27.
30. Mk 16.19, Lk 24.50-51, Acts 1.9, 2.33-36, 1 Pt 3.22, Rom 8.34.
31. Rom 8.34, Heb 9.24, 7.25.
32. Rom 14.9-10, Acts 1.11, 10.42, Mt 13.40-42, Jude 6, 2 Pt 2.4, Mt 16.27, 25.31-33, 2 Tm 4.1, Jn 5.28-29.

5. By his perfect obedience and sacrifice, offered up to God once and for all through the eternal Spirit, the Lord Jesus has completely satisfied the justice of his Father[33] and purchased not only reconciliation but also an everlasting inheritance in the kingdom of heaven for everyone whom the Father has given to him.[34]

33. Rom 5.19, Heb 9.14,16, 10.14, Eph 5.2, Rom 3.25-26.
34. Dn 9.24,26, Col 1.19-20, Eph 1.11,14, Jn 17.2, Heb 9.12,15, Rom 5.10-11, 2 Cor 5.18,20.

6. Although the work of redemption was not actually done by Christ until after his incarnation, yet the power, effectiveness, and benefits of it were given to the elect in all ages from the beginning of the world by means of those promises, types, and sacrifices which revealed him and indicated that he would be the seed of the woman, would bruise the serpent's head, and was the lamb slain from the beginning of the world. Jesus Christ is yesterday and today and forever the same.[35]

   35. Gal 4.4-5, Gn 3.15, Rv 13.8, Heb 13.8; see citations under Chapter 7, Section 5, figures 9 and 10.

7. In the work of mediation Christ acts according to both his natures, each nature doing what is proper to each.[36] However, because of the unity of his person Scripture sometimes attributes what is proper to one nature to the person indicated by the other nature.[37]

   36. Heb 9.14, 1 Pt 3.18, Jn 10.17-18.
   37. Acts 20.28, Jn 3.13, 1 Jn 3.16.

8. Christ insures with absolute certainty that everyone for whom he purchased redemption actually accepts and receives it.[38] He makes intercession for them,[39] reveals the mysteries of salvation to them in and by the word,[40] and effectively persuades them to believe and obey by his Spirit. He governs their hearts by his word and Spirit[41] and overcomes all their enemies by his almighty power and wisdom in such ways as are most in agreement with his wonderful and unknowable administration of things.[42]

   38. Jn 6.37,39, 10.15-16,27-28.
   39. 1 Jn 2.1-2, Rom 8.34.
   40. Jn 15.13,15, Eph 1.7-9, Jn 17.6, Gal 1.11-12.
   41. Jn 14.16, Heb 12.2, 2 Cor 4.13, Rom 8.9,14, 15.18-19, Jn 17.17, Ti 3.4-5.
   42. Ps 110.1, 1 Cor 15.25-26, Mal 4.2-3, Col 2.15, Lk 10.19.

# Chapter 9
## Free Will

1. God has given man a will, which by nature is free, i.e., it is not forced or necessarily inclined toward good or evil.[1]

   1. Mt 17.12, Jas 1.14, Dt 30.19, Jn 5.40, 7.17, Rv 22.17, Acts 7.51, Jas 4.7.

2. In his state of innocence man had complete freedom and the natural ability to will and to do what is good and pleasing to God.[2] God also made man so that he could lose that freedom.[3]

   2. Eccl 7.29, Gn 1.26, see under figure 1 above, Col 3.10.
   3. Gn 2.16-17, 3.6.

3. Man fell into a state of sin by his disobedience and so completely lost his ability to will any spiritual good involving salvation.[4] Consequently fallen man is by nature completely opposed to spiritual good,[5] is dead in sin,[6] and is unable by his own strength either to convert himself or to prepare himself for conversion.[7]

   4. Rom 5.6, 8.7, Jn 15.5.
   5. Rom 3.9-10,12,23, 8.7.
   6. Eph 2.1,5, Col 2.13.
   7. Jn 6.44,65, 1 Cor 2.14, Eph 2.2-5, Ti 3.3-5, Rom 8.8.

4. When God converts a sinner and brings him into a state of grace, he frees him from his natural enslavement to sin. By God's grace alone, freely given, sinful man is enabled to will and to do what is spiritually good.[8] However, since the old sinful nature also remains, the believer cannot consistently or perfectly will to do what is good but also wills evil.[9]

   8. Col 1.13, Jn 8.34,36, Phil 2.13, Rom 6.18,22.
   9. Gal 5.17, Rom 7.15,18-19,21-23, 1 Jn 1.8,10.

## *Free Will*

5. The will of man is perfectly free and permanently inclined to good alone only in the state of glory.[10]

   10. Eph 4.13, Heb 12.23, 1 Jn 3.2, Jude 24, Rv 22.3-4, 2 Chr 6.36, 1 Jn 1.8-10, 2.1-6, Ps 17.15.

# Chapter 10
## Effectual Calling

1. At the right time, appointed by him, God effectually calls all those and only those whom he has predestined to life. He calls them by his word and Spirit out of their natural state of sin and death into grace and salvation through Jesus Christ.[1] He enlightens their minds spiritually with a saving understanding of the things of God.[2] He takes away their hearts of stone and gives them hearts of flesh.[3] He renews their wills and by his almighty power leads them to what is good.[4] And so he effectually draws them to Jesus Christ.[5] But they come to Jesus voluntarily, having been made willing by God's grace.[6]

   1. Rom 8.28,30, 11.7, Eph 1.5,10-11, 2 Thes 2.13-14, 2 Cor 3.3,6, Rom 8.2, 2 Tm 1.9-10, Jn 15.16, Acts 13.48, 1 Thes 5.9, Jas 1.18, 1 Cor 2.12, Eph 2.1-10.
   2. Acts 26.18, 1 Cor 2.10,12, Eph 1.17-18, 2 Cor 4.6.
   3. Ez 36.26.
   4. Ez 11.19, Phil 2.13, Dt 30.6, Ez 36.27, Phil 4.13, Jn 3.5, Gal 6.15, Ti 3.5, 1 Pt 1.23.
   5. Eph 1.19, Jn 6.44-45.
   6. Sg 1.4, Ps 110.3, Jn 6.37, Rom 6.16-18, Mt 11.28, Rv 22.17; see under figure 5 above.

2. This effectual call is freely made by God and is entirely an act of his special grace. It does not depend on anything God foresaw about the person called,[7] who is completely passive. God himself gives life and renewal by the Holy Spirit.[8] He thereby enables each person to answer his call and to accept the grace he offers and actually gives.[9]

   7. 2 Tm 1.9, Ti 3.4-5, Eph 2.4-5,8-9, Rom 9.11.
   8. 1 Cor 2.14, Rom 8.7-9, Eph 2.5.
   9. Jn 6.37, Ez 36.27, Jn 5.25.

3. Elect infants, dying in infancy, are regenerated and saved by Christ, through the Spirit,[10] who works when, where, and how he pleases.[11] The same is true of all other elect persons who are incapable of being outwardly called by the ministry of the word.[12]

> 10. Lk 18.15-16, Acts 2.38-39, Jn 3.3,5-6, 1 Jn 5.12, Rom 8.9, Gn 17.7, Ps 105.8-10, Ez 16.20-21, Gal 3.29, Acts 16.15,31-33, 1 Cor 1.16.
> 11. Jn 3.8.
> 12. 1 Jn 5.12, Acts 4.12, Jn 3.8, 16.7-8.

4. Others, not elect, may be called by the ministry of the word, and the Spirit may work in them in some of the same ways he works in the elect. However, they never truly come to Christ and therefore cannot be saved.[13] And, of course, people, not professing the Christian religion, cannot be saved in any other way at all,[14] no matter how hard they try to live a moral life according to their own understanding or try to obey the rules of some other religion. To say they can be saved is extremely harmful and should be considered a horrible suggestion.[15]

> 13. Mt 22.14, 7.22, 13-15,20-21, Heb 6.4-6, Jn 6.64-66, 8.24, 1 Jn 2.19, Acts 28.24.
> 14. Acts 4.12, Jn 14.6, Eph 2.12-13, Jn 4.22, 17.3.
> 15. 2 Jn 9-11, 1 Cor 16.22, Gal 1.6-8.

# Chapter 11
## Justification

1. Those whom God effectually calls he also freely justifies.[1] He does not pour righteousness into them but pardons their sins and looks on them and accepts them as if they were righteous—not because of anything worked in them or done by them, but for Christ's sake alone. He does not consider their faith itself, the act of believing, as their righteousness or any other obedient response to the gospel on their part. Rather, he imputes to them the obedience and judicial satisfaction earned by Christ.[2] For their part, they receive and rest on Christ and his righteousness by faith (and this faith is not their own but is itself a gift of God).[3]

   1. Rom 8.30, 3.24.
   2. Rom 4.5-8, 2 Cor 5.19,21, Rom 3.22,24-25,27-28, Ti 3.5,7, Eph 1.7, Jer 23.6, 1 Cor 1.30-31, Rom 5.17-19.
   3. Acts 10.43-44, Gal 2.16, Phil 3.9, Acts 13.38-39, Eph 2.7-8, Jn 1.12, 6.44-45, Phil 1.29.

2. Faith, thus receiving and resting on Christ and his righteousness, is the only means of justification.[4] In the person justified, however, it is always accompanied by all the other saving graces and is not a dead faith, but works by love.[5]

   4. Jn 1.12, Rom 3.28, 5.1, Jn 3.16,18,36.
   5. Jas 2.17,22,26, Gal 5.6.

3. By his obedience and death Christ completely discharged the debt of all those who are so justified, and he made the correct, real, and full satisfaction to his Father's justice on their behalf.[6] Since Christ was voluntarily given by the Father for them,[7] and since his obedience and satisfaction were accepted in their place[8] and not for anything in them, their justification is the result only of his free grace[9]—so that both the perfect justice and the rich grace of God might be glorified in the justification of sinners.[10]

> 6. Rom 5.8-10,18-19, 1 Tm 2.5-6, Heb 10.10,14, Dn 9.24,26, Is 53.4-6,10-12, 1 Cor 15.3, 2 Cor 5.21, 1 Pt 2.24, 3.18.
> 7. Rom 8.32, Jn 3.16.
> 8. 2 Cor 5.21, Mt 3.17, Eph 5.2, Is 53.6.
> 9. Rom 3.24, Eph 1.7, Rom 6.23, Eph 2.6-9.
> 10. Rom 3.26, Eph 2.7.

4. From all eternity God decreed the justification of all the elect,[11] and in the fulness of time Christ died for their sins and rose again for their justification.[12] Nevertheless, the elect are not justified until the Holy Spirit in due time does actually apply Christ to them.[13]

> 11. Gal 3.8, 1 Pt 1.2,19-20, Rom 8.30.
> 12. Gal 4.4, 1 Tm 2.6, Rom 4.25, 1 Pt 1.21.
> 13. Col 1.21-22, Gal 2.16, Ti 3.4-7, Jn 3.5,18,36.

5. God continues to forgive the sins of those who are justified.[14] Although they can never fall from the state of justification,[15] they may by their sins come under God's fatherly displeasure and not have a sense of his presence with them until they humble themselves, confess their sins, ask for forgiveness, and renew their faith in repentance.[16]

> 14. Mt 6.12, 1 Jn 1.7,9, 2.1-2.
> 15. Lk 22.32, Jn 10.28, Heb 10.14, Phil 1.6, 1 Jn 2.19; see proofs under Chapter 17.
> 16. Ps 89.31-33, 51.7-12, 32.5, Mt 26.75, 1 Cor 11.30,32, Lk 1.20.

6. The justification of believers under the Old Testament was in all these respects identical with the justification of believers under the New Testament.[17]

> 17. Gal 3.6-9,13-14, Rom 4.22-24, Heb 13.8, 11.13, Jn 8.56, Acts 15.11, Rom 3.30.

# Chapter 12
## Adoption

1. God guarantees the gracious gift of adoption for all those who are justified in and for the sake of his only son, Jesus Christ.[1] Those adopted enjoy the liberties and privileges of God's children,[2] have his name put on them,[3] receive the Spirit of adoption,[4] have access to the throne of grace with boldness,[5] and are enabled to cry, Abba, Father.[6] They are pitied,[7] protected,[8] provided for,[9] and disciplined by him as a father.[10] They are never cast off, however,[11] and are sealed until the day of redemption[12] and inherit the promises[13] as heirs of everlasting salvation.[14]

    1. Eph 1.5, Gal 4.4-5.
    2. Rom 8.17, Jn 1.12.
    3. Jer 14.9, 2 Cor 6.18, Rv 3.12.
    4. Rom 8.15.
    5. Eph 3.12, Rom 5.2, Heb 4.16.
    6. Gal 4.6.
    7. Ps 103.13.
    8. Prv 14.26, Ps 27.1-3.
    9. Mt 6.30,32, 1 Pt 5.7.
    10. Heb 12.6.
    11. Lam 3.31-32, Heb 13.5.
    12. Eph 4.30.
    13. Heb 6.12.
    14. 1 Pt 1.3-4, Heb 1.14.

# Chapter 13
## Sanctification

1. Those who are effectually called and regenerated have a new heart and a new spirit created in them. They are additionally sanctified, actually and personally, by the power of Christ's death and resurrection and by his word and Spirit dwelling in them.[1] The power of sin ruling over the whole body is destroyed,[2] and the desires of the old self are more and more weakened and killed.[3] At the same time the ability to practice true holiness, without which no one will see the Lord,[4] is brought to life and strengthened by all the saving graces.[5]

   1. 1 Cor 6.11, Acts 20.32, Phil 3.10, Rom 6.5-6, Jn 17.17,19, Eph 5.26, 2 Thes 2.13, 1 Cor 1.30.
   2. Rom 6.6,14.
   3. Gal 5.24, Rom 8.13, Col 3.5.
   4. 2 Cor 7.1, Heb 12.14, Col 1.28, 4.12.
   5. Col 1.10-11, Eph 3.16-19, 2 Pt 3.13-14.

2. This sanctification works in the whole person,[6] but not completely or perfectly in this life. The old sinful nature retains some of its control in body, mind, and spirit. And so a continual and irreconcilable war goes on in every believer. The old nature tries to get its way in opposition to the Spirit, and the Spirit fights to assert authority over the flesh.[7]

   6. 1 Thes 5.23.
   7. 1 Jn 1.10, Rom 7.18,23, Phil 3.12, Gal 5.17, 1 Pt 2.11.

## Sanctification

3. Although the old nature temporarily wins battles in this warfare,[8] the continual strengthening of the sanctifying Spirit of Christ enables the regenerate nature in each believer to overcome.[9] And so believers grow in grace,[10] perfecting holiness in the fear of God.[11]

8. Rom 7.23.
9. Rom 6.14, 1 Jn 5.4, Eph 4.15-16.
10. 2 Pt 3.18, 2 Cor 3.18.
11. 2 Cor 7.1.

# Chapter 14
## Saving Faith

1. The gift of faith makes it possible for the souls of the elect to be saved by believing in Jesus Christ. This gift is the work of the Spirit of Christ in the hearts of the elect[1] and is ordinarily accomplished by the ministry of the word.[2] It is also increased and strengthened by the word, by prayer, and by the administration of the sacraments.[3]

   1. Heb 10.39, 2 Cor 4.13, Eph 1.17-20, 2.8, 1 Cor 12.3, Heb 12.2; see proofs under Chapter 11.
   2. Rom 10.14,17, Mt 28.19-20, 1 Cor 1.21.
   3. 1 Pt 2.2, Acts 20.32, Rom 4.11, Lk 17.5, Rom 1.16-17, Mt 28.19, 1 Cor 11.23-29, 2 Cor 12.8-10, Lk 22.19, Jn 6.54-56, Lk 22.32.

2. By this faith a Christian believes whatever is revealed in the word to be the true, authentic, authoritative statement of God himself.[4] By this faith the believer also acts according to what particular passages in the word say. By faith the believer humbly submits to and obeys God's various commands.[5] He trembles at God's awesome threats,[6] and eagerly embraces his promises about this life and the life to come.[7] But the chief actions of saving faith are accepting, receiving, and resting on Christ alone for justification, sanctification, and eternal life, in the power of the covenant of grace.[8]

   4. Jn 4.42, 1 Thes 2.13, 1 Jn 5.10, Acts 24.14.
   5. Rom 16.26, Mt 22.37-40.
   6. Is 66.2.
   7. Heb 11.13, 1 Tm 4.8.
   8. Jn 1.12, Acts 16.31, Gal 2.20, Acts 15.11.

3. This faith has different degrees of strength and weakness.[9] It may be attacked and weakened often and in many ways, but it gets the victory.[10] In many believers it matures and becomes completely assured through Christ,[11] who both creates and perfects our faith.[12]

   9. Heb 5.13-14, Rom 4.19-20, Mt 6.30, 8.10.
   10. Lk 22.31-32, Eph 6.16, 1 Jn 5.4-5, 1 Cor 10.13.
   11. Heb 6.11-12, 10.22, Col 2.2, 2 Tm 1.12; see proofs under Chapter 18.
   12. Heb 12.2.

# Chapter 15
## Repentance Leading to Life

1. Repentance which leads to life is the blessed product of the gospel working in believers' lives.[1] Along with the doctrine of faith in Christ, it is a doctrine to be preached by every minister of the gospel.[2]

   > 1. Zec 12.10, Acts 11.18.
   > 2. Lk 24.47, Mk 1.15, Acts 20.21.

2. In this repentance the sinner is able to see his sins as God sees them, as filthy and hateful, and as involving great danger to the sinner, because they are completely contrary to the holy nature and righteous law of God. Understanding that God in Christ is merciful to those who repent, the sinner suffers deep sorrow for and hates his sins, and so he determines to turn away from all of them. And turning to God,[3] he tries to walk with him according to all his commandments.[4]

   > 3. Ez 18.30-31, 36.31, Is 30.22, Ps 51.4, Jer 31.18-19, Jl 2.12-13,, Am 5.15, Ps 119.128, 2 Cor 7.11.
   > 4. Ps 119.6,59,106, Lk 1.6, 2 Kgs 23.25, Jn 14.23, Mt 21.28-29.

3. Although repentance is not any satisfaction for sin and does not cause the forgiveness of sins[5] (since forgiveness is an act of God's voluntary grace in Christ[6]), yet it is necessary to all sinners, and no one may expect to be forgiven without it.[7]

   > 5. Ez 36.31-32, 16.61-63, Ti 3.5, Acts 5.31.
   > 6. Hos 14.2,4, Rom 3.24, Eph 1.7.
   > 7. Lk 13.3,5, Acts 17.30-31.

## *Repentance Leading to Life*

4. Just as there is no sin so small that it does not deserve damnation,[8] so there is no sin so great that it can bring damnation upon those who truly repent.[9]

> 8. Rom 6.23, 5.12, Mt 12.36, Jas 2.10.
> 9. Is 55.7, Rom 8.1, Is 1.16,18.

5. Believers should not be satisfied with general repentance. Rather, it is everyone's duty to try to repent of every individual sin individually.[10]

> 10. Ps 19.13, Lk 19.8, 1 Tm 1.13,15, Dn 9, Neh 9.

6. Everyone is also bound to confess privately his sins to God and to pray for forgiveness for them.[11] Confession, prayer for forgiveness, and the forsaking of sins which have been forgiven will find God's mercy.[12] Similarly, anyone who sins against his spiritual brother or the church should be willing to confess, privately or publicly, to demonstrate sorrow for his sin, and openly to state his repentance to those whom he has hurt.[13] They in turn are to be reconciled to him and to receive him in love.[14]

> 11. Ps 51.4-5,7,9,14, 32.5-6.
> 12. Prv 28.13, 1 Jn 1.9.
> 13. Jas 5.16, Lk 17.3-4, Jos 7.19, Ps 51.
> 14. 2 Cor 2.7-8, Gal 6.1-2.

# Chapter 16
## Good Works

1. Good works are only those works identified as good by God and commanded by him in his holy word.[1] They do not include other works, no matter how well-intentioned in design or zealously promoted by men.[2]

    1. Mi 6.8, Rom 12.2, Heb 13.21, Dt 12.32, Ps 119.9, Mt 28.20, Lk 10.25-26, 2 Pt 1.19.
    2. Mt 15.9, Is 29.13, 1 Pt 1.18, Rom 10.2, Jn 16.2, 1 Sm 15.21-23, Col 2.16-17,20-23, Dt 10.12-13.

2. These good works, done in obedience to God's commandments, are the fruit and evidence of a true and living faith.[3] By them believers show their thankfulness,[4] strengthen their assurance of salvation,[5] edify their brothers in the Lord,[6] and become ornaments of all those who profess the gospel.[7] Good works in believers silence the criticism of the enemies of the gospel.[8] They also glorify God[9] by showing that believers are the workmanship and creation of Jesus Christ,[10] because their aim is that holiness of living which leads to eternal life.[11]

    3. Jas 2.18,22.
    4. Ps 116.12-13, 1 Pt 2.9, Col 3.17, 1 Chr 29.6-9.
    5. 1 Jn 2.3,5, 2 Pt 1.5-10.
    6. 2 Cor 9.2, Mt 5.16, 1 Tm 4.12.
    7. Ti 2.5,9-12, 1 Tm 6.1.
    8. 1 Pt 2.15.
    9. 1 Pt 2.12, Phil 1.11, Jn 15.8.
    10. Eph 2.10.
    11. Rom 6.22.

# Good Works

3. Believers get the ability to do good works entirely from the Spirit of Christ.[12] In addition to the other particular effects of God's grace already received, believers must be directed by the Holy Spirit in order to will and to do what pleases God.[13] However, they are not therefore to grow spiritually lazy, waiting for some special guidance from the Spirit before doing anything commanded by God. Rather, they should diligently attempt to identify what good works God has commanded in his word and then try their best to do all of them, praying earnestly and daily for the empowering and enabling of the Holy Spirit, who lives in them.[14]

> 12. Jn 15.4-6, Ez 36.26-27, Lk 11.13.
> 13. Phil 2.13, 4.13, 2 Cor 3.5, Eph 3.16.
> 14. Phil 2.12, Heb 6.11-12, 2 Pt 1.3,5,10-11, Is 64.7,
>     2 Tm 1.6, Acts 26.6-7, Jude 20-21.

4. Those believers who do the best that can be done in obeying God in this life can never do more or even as much as he requires. Indeed they fall short of much which they are bound to do.[15]

> 15. Lk 17.10, Neh 13.22, Jb 9.2-3, Gal 5.17.

# Good Works

5. We cannot, of course, by our best works deserve to be forgiven for our sins and to receive eternal life from God. There is that great disproportion between our best works in this life and the glory which is going to be revealed in us, and there is the infinite distance between us and God, who does not profit from our best works and is not satisfied by them for the debt of our previous sins.[16] When we have done all we can, we have only done our duty and are unprofitable servants.[17] Since the goodness of our best works in fact proceeds from his Spirit[18] and since, insofar as they are done by us, our best works are defiled and mixed with our weakness and imperfection, they cannot therefore even stand the scrutiny of God's judgment.[19]

> 16. Rom 3.20, 4.2,4,6, Eph 2.8-9, Ti 3.5-7,
>     Rom 8.18,22-24, Ps 16.2, Jb 22.2-3, 35.7-8.
> 17. Lk 17.10; Gal 5.17.
> 18. Gal 5.22-23.
> 19. Is 64.6, Gal 5.17, Rom 7.15,18, Ps 143.2, 130.3.

6. Nevertheless, since the persons of believers are accepted through Christ, their good works in this life are also accepted in him.[20] It is not as though they were perfect in God's sight[21] but that God, looking on them in his Son, is pleased to accept and reward what is sincerely done, even though accompanied by much weakness and imperfection.[22]

> 20. Eph 1.6, 1 Pt 2.5, Ex 28.38, Gn 4.4, Heb 11.4.
> 21. Jb 9.20, Ps 143.2, 1 Cor 4.3-4.
> 22. Heb 13.20-21, 2 Cor 8.12, Heb 6.10, Mt 25.21,23.

## Good Works

7. Works done by people who have not been spiritually reborn may be the same as those commanded by God and may be of good use to them and to others.[23] However, since they do not proceed from a heart purified by faith, [24] are not done in the right way, i.e., in response to God's word,[25] and are not done for the right purpose, the glory of God,[26] they are therefore sinful and cannot please God or make a person fit to receive grace from God.[27] Nevertheless, it is more sinful and displeasing to God not to do such works than to do them.[28]

23. 2 Kgs 10.30-31, 1 Kgs 21.27,29, Phil 1.15-16,18.
24. Gn 4.3-5, Heb 11.4,6.
25. 1 Cor 13.3, Is 1.12, Mk 10.20-21.
26. Mt 6.2,5,16, Rom 14.23.
27. Hg 2.14, Ti 1.15, Am 5.21-22, Hos 1.4, Rom 9.16, Ti 3.5, Prv 15.8, 28.9, Mk 7.6-7.
28. Ps 14.4, 36.3, Jb 21.14-15, Mt 25.41-45, 23.23, 25.24-28.

# Chapter 17
## The Perseverance of Christians

1. Those whom God has accepted in his Son and has effectually called and sanctified by his Spirit can never completely or finally fall out of their state of grace. Rather, they shall definitely continue in that state to the end and are eternally saved.[1]

   1. Phil 1.6, 2 Pt 1.10, Jn 10.28-29, 1 Jn 3.9, 1 Pt 1.5,9, Jb 17.9, Jer 32.40.

2. This endurance of Christians does not depend on their own free will but on God's unchangeable decree of election, flowing from his voluntary, unchangeable love.[2] It also depends on the effectiveness of the merit and intercession of Jesus Christ,[3] on the indwelling Spirit and indwelling seed of God in believers,[4] and on the nature of the covenant of grace.[5] All these establish the certainty and infallibility of their preservation.[6]

   2. 2 Tm 2.18-19, Jer 31.3, Eph 1.4-5, Jn 13.1, Rom 8.35-39.
   3. Heb 10.10,14, 13.20-21, 9.12-15, Rom 8.32-39, Jn 17.11,24, Lk 22.32, Heb 7.25.
   4. Jn 14.16-17, 1 Jn 2.27, 3.9.
   5. Jer 32.40, Heb 8.10-12.
   6. Jn 10.28, 2 Thes 3.3, 1 Jn 2.19, 1 Thes 5.23-24, Heb 6.17-20.

3. Nevertheless, the temptations of Satan, the world, and their old carnal natures, along with neglect of the means of their preservation, may lead believers to commit serious sins and to continue in them for a time.[7] They consequently displease God[8] and grieve his Holy Spirit,[9] have some of the fruit of God's grace and his comforts taken away from them,[10] have their hearts hardened[11] and their consciences wounded,[12] hurt and offend others,[13] and bring temporal judgments on themselves.[14]

7. Mt 26.70,72,74, Ps 51.Title and verse 14, 2 Sm 12.9,13.
8. Is 64.5,7,9, 2 Sm 11.27.
9. Eph 4.30.
10. Ps 51.8,10,12, Rv 2.4, Sg 5.2-4,6.
11. Is 36.17, Mk 6.52, 16.14, Ps 95.8.
12. Ps 32.3-4, 51.8.
13. 2 Sm 12.14, Ez 16.54.
14. Ps 89.31-32, 1 Cor 11.32, 2 Sm 12.10.

# Chapter 18
## The Assurance of Grace and Salvation

1. Hypocrites and other unregenerate men may deceive themselves with false hopes and carnal presumptions about their being in God's favor and about their being saved.[1] Their presumptions will die with them.[2] However, those who truly believe in the Lord Jesus, who honestly love him and try to walk in good conscience before him, may in this life be assured with certainty that they are in a state of grace.[3] They may also rejoice in the hope of the glory of God, and they will never be ashamed of that hope.[4]

> 1. Jb 8.13-14, Mi 3.11, Dt 29.19, Jn 8.41.
> 2. Mt 7.22-23, Jb 8.13.
> 3. 1 Jn 2.3, 3.14,18-19,21,24, 5.13, 2 Tm 1.12.
> 4. Rom 5.2,5; see citations under 3 above; 2 Tm 4.7-8.

2. This certainty is not based on the fallible hope of guesswork or probabilities. Rather, it is the infallible assurance of faith,[5] established on the divine truth of the promises of salvation.[6] There is also the inner evidence of spiritual insight, given to us by God, to which these promises are directed.[7] And there is the testimony of the Spirit of adoption, witnessing with our spirits that we are the children of God.[8] This Spirit is the pledge of our inheritance. By him we are sealed until the day of redemption.[9]

> 5. Heb 6.11-12,19; see citations under 3 and 4 above.
> 6. Heb 6.17-18, 2 Pt 1.4-5.
> 7. 2 Pt 1.4-5,10-11, 1 Jn 2.3, 3.14, 2 Cor 1.12.
> 8. Rom 8.15-16.
> 9. Eph 1.13-14, 4.30, 2 Cor 1.21-22.

# The Assurance of Grace and Salvation

3. This infallible assurance is not so essential to faith that a true believer may not have doubts and conflicts about it, possibly wait some time for it, and grow into it.[10] But since the Spirit enables believers to know the things which are freely given to them by God, every believer may come to a full assurance of salvation by the ordinary working of the Spirit without unusual revelation.[11] Therefore it is every believer's duty to establish the certainty of his calling and election[12] so that his heart may be filled with peace and joy in the Holy Spirit, with love and thankfulness to God, and with strength and cheerfulness of obedience. These are the true products of assurance,[13] which is never conducive to an undisciplined life.[14]

10. 1 Jn 5.13, Is 50.10, Mk 9.24, Ps 88, 77.1-20, 73.
11. 1 Cor 2.12, 1 Jn 4.13, Heb 6.11-12, Eph 3.17-19,
    Ps 77.10-20, 73, see citations under Section 2 above.
12. 2 Pt 1.10.
13. Rom 5.1-2,5, 14.17, 15.13, Eph 1.3-4,
    Ps 4.6-7, 119.32.
14. 1 Jn 2.1-2, Rom 6.1-2, Ti 2.11-12,14, 2 Cor 7.1,
    Rom 8.1,12, 1 Jn 3.2-3, Ps 130.4, 1 Jn 1.6-7,
    2 Pt 1.10.

# The Assurance of Grace and Salvation

4. The assurance true believers have of their salvation may be shaken, lessened, or interrupted for various reasons: from neglecting to preserve it; from committing some particular sin, which wounds the conscience and grieves the Spirit; from some sudden or strong temptation; or from God's withdrawing the sense of his presence and allowing them to walk in darkness.[15] Nevertheless, they are never completely without God's seed, the life of faith, the love of Christ and of other believers, and the sincere heart and obedient conscience, out of which the Spirit may revive this assurance in due time[16] and by which they are in the meantime kept from complete despair.[17]

15. Sg 5.2-3,6, Ps 51.8,12,14, Eph 4.30-31, Ps 77.1-10, Mt 26.69-72, Ps 31.22, Ps 88, Is 50.10.
16. 1 Jn 3.9, Lk 22.32, Jb 13.15, Ps 73.15, Ps 51.8,12, Is 50.10.
17. Mi 7.7-9, Jer 52.40, Is 54.7-10, Ps 22.1, 88, 2 Cor 4.8-10.

# Chapter 19
## The Law of God

1. God gave Adam a law as a covenant of works. He required Adam and all his descendants to obey this law, individually, completely, perpetually, and in precise accordance with its provisions. God promised life for keeping it and threatened death for disobeying it, and he gave man the power and ability to keep it.[1]

   1. Gn 1.26-27, 2.17, Rom 2.14-15, 10.5, 5.12,19,
      Gal 3.10,12, Eccl 7.29, Jb 28.28, Eph 4.24.

2. After the fall this law continued to be a perfect rule of righteousness and was given, as such, by God on Mount Sinai in the Ten Commandments, written on two tablets.[2] The first four commandments establish our obligations to God and the remaining six our obligations to human beings.[3]

   2. Jas 1.25, 2.8,10-12, Rom 13.8-9, Dt 5.32, 10.4,
      Ex 34.1, Rom 3.19, Gal 3.12, Hos 6.7, Gn 2.16-17;
      compare Rom 5.12-14, 1 Cor 15.22, Lk 10.25-28, and
      the covenants made with Noah and Abraham;
      Gn 1.26, Dt 30.19, Jn 7.17, Rv 22.17, Jas 1.14.
   3. Mt 22.37-40, Ex 20.3-18.

# The Law of God

3. In addition to this law, ordinarily called the moral law, it pleased God to give the people of Israel, as a pre-Christian assembly of believers, ceremonial laws, containing many typical ordinances. Some of these ordinances pertain to worship and foreshadow Christ, his grace, actions, suffering, and the benefits to be had from believing in him.[4] The rest of these ordinances contain various instructions about moral duties.[5] All of these ceremonial laws are now nullified under the New Testament.[6]

> 4. Heb 9, 10.1, Gal 4.1-3, Col 2.17.
> 5. 1 Cor 5.7, 2 Cor 6.17, Jude 23; see Lv 5.1-6, 6.1-7, and similar passages, Ex 12.14.
> 6. Col 2.14,16-17, Dn 9.27, Eph 2.15-16, Mk 7.18-19, Gal 2.4.

4. God also gave the Israelites, as a political body, various judicial laws. These expired with the state of Israel and make no further obligation on God's people than seems appropriate in contemporary legal codes.[7]

> 7. Ex 21, 22.1-29, Gn 49.10, 1 Pt 2.13-14, Mt 5.17,38-39, 1 Cor 9.8-10.

5. The moral law, however, does pertain to everyone, saved and unsaved, forever, not just with respect to its content but also in relationship to the authority of God, the Creator, who gave it.[8] In the gospel Christ does not in any way remove this obligation, but rather strengthens it.[9]

> 8. Rom 13.8-10, Eph 6.2, 1 Jn 2.3-4,7-8, Rom 3.31, 6.15, Jas 2.8,10-11; see citations under Section 2 above, Rom 3.19.
> 9. Mt 5.17-19, Jas 2.8, Rom 3.31.

# The Law of God

6. Although true believers are not justified or condemned by the law as a covenant of works,[10] the law is nevertheless very useful to them and to others. As a rule of life, it informs them of God's will and of their obligation to obey it.[11] It also reveals to them the sinful pollution of their nature, hearts, and lives,[12] so that, examining themselves from its point of view, they may become more convinced of the presence of sin in them, more humiliated on account of that sin, and hate sin the more.[13] Thus they gain a better awareness of their need for Christ and for the perfection of his obedience.[14] The prohibitions against sin[15] in the law are also useful in restraining believers from pursuing the desires of their old nature, and the punishments for disobedience in the law show them what their sins deserve and what afflictions they may expect for them in this life, even though they have been freed from the curse threatened in the law.[16] The promises of the law similarly show them that God approves obedience and that blessings may be expected for obedience,[17] although not as their due from the law as a covenant of works.[18] The fact that the law encourages doing good and discourages doing evil does not mean that a person who does good and refrains from evil is under the law and not under grace.[19]

10. Rom 6.14, Gal 2.16, 3.13, 4.4-5, Acts 13.39, Rom 8.1.
11. Rom 7.12,22,25, Ps 119.4-6, 1 Cor 7.19, Gal 5.14,16,18-23.
12. Rom 7.7, 3.20.
13. Jas 1.23-25, Rom 7.9,14,24.
14. Gal 3.24, Rom 7.24-25, 8.3-4.
15. Jas 2.11, Ps 119.101,104,128.
16. Ezr 9.13-14, Ps 89.30-34.
17. Lv 26.1-14, 2 Cor 6.16, Eph 6.2-3, Ps 37.11, Mt 5.5, Ps 19.11.
18. Gal 2.16, Lk 17.10.
19. Rom 6.12,14, 1 Pt 3.8-12, Ps 34.12-16, Heb 12.28-29.

7. None of these uses of the law is contrary to the grace of the gospel. They rather beautifully comply with it,[20] because the Spirit of Christ subdues and enables the will of man to do voluntarily and cheerfully what the will of God, revealed in the law, requires to be done.[21]

   20. Gal 3.21, Ti 2.11-14; see citations under Section 6 above.
   21. Ez 36.27, Heb 8.10, Jer 31.33; see citations under Chapter 10 Section 1, Gal 3.13.

# Chapter 20
## Christian Freedom and Freedom of Conscience

1. Christ has purchased for believers under the gospel freedom from the guilt of sin, from the condemning wrath of God, and from the curse of the moral law.[1] He has also freed them from the evil world we live in, from enslavement to Satan, from the dominion of sin,[2] the evil of afflictions, the sting of death, the victory of the grave, and from everlasting damnation.[3] In Christ believers have free access to God[4] and can obey him, not out of slavish fear, but with a childlike love and a willing mind.[5] All these freedoms were also held by believers under the law.[6] However, under the New Testament, the liberty of Christians has been enlarged to include freedom from the yoke of the ceremonial law, to which the Jewish church was subjected.[7] Christians also have greater boldness of access to the throne of grace[8] and a fuller gift of the Spirit of God than believers ordinarily had under the law.[9]

   1. Ti 2.14, 1 Thes 1.10, Gal 3.13, Rom 8.1.
   2. Gal 1.4, Col 1.13, Acts 26.18, Rom 6.14, 1 Jn 1.7.
   3. Rom 8.28, Ps 119.71, 1 Cor 15.54-57, Rom 8.1.
   4. Rom 5.1-2, Eph 2.18, 3.12, Heb 10.19.
   5. Rom 8.14-15, 1 Jn 4.18, Eph 2.18, Gal 4.6, Heb 10.19.
   6. Gal 3.9,14; see citations under Chapter 8, Section 6.
   7. Gal 4.1-3,6-7, 5.1, Acts 15.10-11.
   8. Heb 4.14,16, 10.19-22.
   9. Jn 7.38-39, 2 Cor 3.13,17-18, Rom 5.5.

# Christian Freedom and Freedom of Conscience

2. God alone is Lord of the conscience and has left it free from the doctrines and commandments of men which are in any way contrary to or different from his word in matters of faith or worship.[10] And so, believing any such teachings or obeying any such commandments of men for conscience's sake actually betrays true freedom of conscience.[11] Requiring implicit or absolute, blind obedience also destroys freedom of conscience as well as the free use of reason.[12]

> 10. Jas 4.12, Rom 14.4,10, Acts 4.19, 5.29, 1 Cor 7.23, Mt 23.8-10, 2 Cor 1.24, Mt 15.9.
> 11. Col 2.20-23, Gal 1.10, 5.1, 2.3-5, Ps 5.1, Gal 4.9-10.
> 12. Rom 10.17, 14.23, Is 8.20, Acts 17.11, Jn 4.22, Hos 5.11, Rv 13.12,16-17, Jer 8.9, 1 Pt 3.15.

3. Those who practice any sin or nourish any sinful desire on the pretext of Christian freedom destroy the whole purpose of Christian freedom, which is, that, having been rescued out of the hands of our enemies, we might serve the Lord without fear and in holiness and righteousness before him all the days of our lives.[13]

> 13. Gal 5.13, 1 Pt 2.16, 2 Pt 2.19, Jn 8.34, Lk 1.74-75, Rom 6.15, 2 Pt 3.15.

# Christian Freedom and Freedom of Conscience

4. God intends that the authorities he has ordained on earth and the freedom Christ has purchased should not destroy but mutually uphold and preserve each other. And so, those who oppose any lawful power or the lawful exercise of power, whether civil or ecclesiastical, on the pretext of Christian freedom, are actually resisting God.[14] The support, promotion, or practice of such opposition, which contradicts natural understanding or the known principles of Christianity on matters of faith, worship, and associations, which denies the power of godliness, or which disrupts the peace and unity among believers, may lawfully be called to account and proceeded against by the church.[15]

14. Mt 12.25, 1 Pt 2.13-14,16, Rom 13.1-8, Heb 13.17.
15. Rom 1.32, 1 Cor 5.1,5,11-13, 2 Jn 5.10-11,
    2 Thes 3.14, 1 Tm 6.3-5, Ti 1.10-11,13, 3.10,
    Mt 18.15-18, 1 Tm 1.19-20, Rv 2.14-15,20, 3.9,
    Rom 16.17, 2 Thes 3.6, Dt 13.6-12, Rom 13.3-4,
    2 Jn 5.10-11, Ezr 7.23-28, Rv 17.12,16-17,
    Neh 13.15,17,21- 22,25,30, 2 Kgs 23.5-6,9,20-21,
    2 Chr 34.33, 15.12-13,16, Dn 3.29, 1 Tm 2.2,
    Is 49.23, Zech 13.2-3.

# Chapter 21
## Religious Worship and the Sabbath Day

1. Natural understanding reveals that there is a God, who is lord and sovereign over everything, who is good and does good to everyone, and who is therefore to be held in awe, loved, praised, called upon, trusted in, and served with all our heart, soul, and might.[1] The acceptable way of worshiping the true God is established by God himself. God's revealed will so defines and outlines proper worship that neither the imaginations and devices of men nor the suggestions of Satan are to be followed. God is not to be worshiped under any visible representation or in any other way than that prescribed in Holy Scripture.[2]

   1. Rom 1.19-20, Acts 17.24, Ps 119.68, Jer 10.7, Ps 31.23, 18.3, Rom 10.12, Ps 62.8, Jos 24.14, Mk 12.33, Ps 19.1-6, Acts 14.17.
   2. Dt 12.32, Mt 15.9, Acts 17.24-25, Mt 4.9-10, Dt 4.15-20, Ex 20.4-6, Col 2.20-23, Jn 4.23-24.

2. Religious worship is to be given to God, the Father, Son, and Holy Spirit, and only to him,[3] but not to angels, saints, or any other creatures.[4] Since the fall this worship must involve a mediator, and there is no other mediator than Christ alone.[5]

   3. Mt 4.10, Jn 5.23, 2 Cor 13.14, Rv 5.11-14, Mt 28.19.
   4. Col 2.18, Rv 19.10, Rom 1.25.
   5. Jn 14.6, 1 Tm 2.5, Eph 2.18, Col 3.17.

3. Prayer with thanksgiving is one part of religious worship[6] and is required by God from all men.[7] In order for prayer to be accepted, it must be made in the name of Jesus,[8] by the help of his Spirit,[9] according to his will,[10] with understanding, reverence, humility, fervor, faith, love, and perseverance,[11] and, if vocal, in a known tongue.[12]

> 6. Phil 4.6, 1 Tm 2.1, Col 4.2.
> 7. Ps 65.2, Lk 18.1, 1 Tm 2.8, Ps 67.3, 1 Thes 5.17-18.
> 8. Jn 14.13-14, 1 Pt 2.5.
> 9. Rom 8.26, Eph 6.18.
> 10. 1 Jn 5.14.
> 11. Ps 47.7, Eccl 5.1-2, Heb 12.28, Gn 18.27,
>     Jas 5.16, 1.6-7, Mk 11.24, Mt 6.12,14-15, Col 4.2,
>     Eph 6.18.
> 12. 1 Cor 14.14.

4. Prayer is to be made for lawful things[13] and for people who are alive or may be born,[14] but not for the dead,[15] nor for those who are known to have committed the sin unto death.[16]

> 13. 1 Jn 5.14, Mt 26.42.
> 14. 1 Tm 2.1-2, Jn 17.20, 2 Sm 7.29, Ru 4.12.
> 15. 2 Sm 12.21-23, Lk 16.25-26, Rv 14.13; this statement
>     is based on the absence of any command to pray for
>     the dead, and of any example in the Scripture of
>     such prayer, 1 Jn 5.14.
> 16. 1 Jn 5.16.

5. The ordinary worship of God includes: the reverent and attentive reading of the Scriptures,[17] the sound preaching[18] and conscientious hearing of the word in obedience to God with understanding and faith;[19] singing of psalms with grace in the heart;[20] and the proper administration and right receiving of the sacraments instituted by Christ.[21] Then there are religious oaths[22] and vows,[23] solemn fasting,[24] and thanksgiving on special occasions.[25] Worship should include these at appropriate times, and they should be performed in a holy and religious manner.[26]

17. Acts 15.21, Rv 1.3, Acts 17.11.
18. 2 Tm 4.2.
19. Jas 1.22, Acts 10.33, Mt 13.19, Heb 4.2, Is 66.2.
20. Col 3.16, Eph 5.19, Jas 5.13, Acts 16.25.
21. Mt 28.19, 1 Cor 11.23-29, Acts 2.42.
22. Dt 6.13, Neh 10.29.
23. Is 19.21, Eccl 5.4-5, Acts 18.18, Ps 116.14, Neh 10.29.
24. Jl 2.12, Est 4.16, Mt 9.15, 1 Cor 7.5, Mt 6.17-18.
25. Ps 107, Est 9.22, Neh 12.31-43.
26. Heb 12.28, Jn 4.24, Heb 10.22.

6. Under the gospel neither prayer nor any other part of religious worship is tied to or made more acceptable by being performed in any particular place.[27] God is to be worshiped everywhere[28] in spirit and in truth;[29] in private families[30] daily;[31] privately by individuals daily;[32] and regularly in solemn public gatherings, which are not to be carelessly or willfully neglected or forsaken, since God calls us to join other believers in public worship.[33]

> 27. Jn 4.21.
> 28. Mal 1.11, 1 Tm 2.8.
> 29. Jn 4.23-24.
> 30. Jer 10.25, Dt 6.6-7, Jb 1.5, 2 Sm 6.8-18,20, 1 Pt 3.7, Acts 10.2.
> 31. Mt 6.11, Jos 24.15, Dn 6.10.
> 32. Mt 6.6, Eph 6.18, Neh 1.4-11.
> 33. Is 56.7, Heb 10.25, Prv 1.20-21,24, 8.34, Acts 13.42, Lk 4.16, Acts 2.42.

7. It is a law of our natural, earthly life that some appropriate amount of time be set aside for the worship of God. In his word God has similarly commanded all men in every age to keep one day in seven holy unto him as a sabbath.[34] From the beginning of the world up to the resurrection of Christ, this sabbath was the last day of the week. Since the resurrection of Christ it has been changed to the first day of the week, called the Lord's day in Scripture, and is to be continued until the end of the world as the Christian sabbath.[35]

> 34. Ex 20.8-11, Is 56.2,4,6-7.
> 35. Gn 2.2-3, 1 Cor 16.1-2, Acts 20.7, Rv 1.10, Ex 20.8,10, Mt 5.17-18; these texts are cited in connection with the example of the apostles and the early church.

8. The sabbath is kept holy unto the Lord when men prepare their hearts for it; arrange for their daily affairs to be taken care of beforehand; rest the whole day from their own works and words, and from thoughts about their wordly activities and recreations;[36] and take up the whole time in public and private worship and in the duties of necessity and mercy.[37]

    36. Ex 20.8, 16.23,25-26,29-30, 31.15-17, Is 58.13, Neh 13.15-22, Lk 23.56.
    37. Is 58.13, Mt 12.1-13.

# Chapter 22
## Lawful Oaths and Vows

1. Lawful oaths are part of religious worship.[1] On proper occasions believers may solemnly swear and call God to witness that what they assert or promise is true, and they may ask God to judge them according to the truth or falsehood of what they swear.[2]

    1. Dt 10.20.
    2. Ex 20.7, Lv 19.12, 2 Cor 1.23, 2 Chr 6.22-23

2. The name of God is the only name by which men should swear, and that name is to be used with holy awe and reverence.[3] Therefore to swear vainly or rashly by that glorious and mighty name or to swear at all by any other name is sinful and should be considered a horrible thing to do.[4] Just as in important matters an oath is warranted by the word of God, under the New as well as the Old Testament, so a lawful oath, required by legitimate authority in such matters ought to be taken.[5]

    3. Dt 6.13.
    4. Ex 20.7, Jer 5.7, Mt 5.34,37, Jas 5.12.
    5. Heb 6.16, 2 Cor 1.23, Is 65.16, 1 Kgs 8.31, Neh 13.25, Ezr 10.5, Mt 26.63-64.

3. Whoever takes an oath ought to consider fully the importance of such a solemn act, and so he should swear to nothing but what he is completely convinced is true. No one may bind himself by an oath to anything but what is good and just, to what he believes to be true, and to what he is able and determined to perform. It is a sin to refuse to swear an oath about anything good and just, when it is required by lawful authority.[6]

    6. Ex 20.7, Jer 4.2, Gn 24.2-3,5-6,8-9, Nm 5.19,21, Neh 5.12, Ex 22.7-11; see citations under Section 2 above.

4. An oath is to be taken in the plain, ordinary sense of the words used, without any equivocation or mental reservation.[7] It cannot obligate one to sin; but once taken about anything not sinful, it must be performed, even to one's own harm,[8] and must not be broken, even if made to heretics or atheists.[9]

> 7. Jer 4.2, Ps 24.4, Ex 20.7.
> 8. 1 Sm 25.22,32-34, Ps 15.4.
> 9. Ez 17.16,18-19, Jos 9.18-19, 2 Sm 21.1.

5. A vow is similar to an oath promising something and should be made with similar religious care and performed with similar faithfulness.[10]

> 10. Is 19.21, Eccl 5.4-6, Ps 61.8, 66.13-14, Dt 23.21,23.

6. A vow should be made to no one but God.[11] In order to be accepted it should be made voluntarily in a faithful and conscientious way as thanks for mercy received or as means of getting what we want. A vow binds us more strictly to necessary duties or to other things to such an extent and for as long as is appropriate.[12]

> 11. Ps 76.11, Jer 44.25-26.
> 12. Dt 23.21,23, Ps 50.14, Gn 28.20-22, 1 Sm 1.11,
>     Ps 66.13-14, 132.2-5.

7. No one may vow to do anything forbidden in the word of God, anything hindering a duty commanded in the word, or anything not in his own power, which he has neither the ability nor warrant from God to perform.[13] In this respect monastic vows of perpetual celibacy, professed poverty, and consistent obedience do not perfect us but are actually superstitious, sinful traps, in which no Christian should entangle himself.[14]

> 13. Acts 23.12,14, Mk 6.26, Nm 30.5,8,12-13.
> 14. Mt 19.11-12, 1 Cor 7.2,9, Eph 4.28, 1 Pt 4.2,
>     1 Cor 7.23, 1 Thes 4.11-12.

# Chapter 23
## Civil Authorities

1. God, the supreme Lord and King of the whole world, has ordained civil authorities to be over people under him for his own glory and the public good. For this purpose he has armed civil authorities with the power of the sword to defend and encourage those who are good and to punish wrongdoers.[1]

   1. Rom 13.1-4, 1 Pt 2.13-14

2. It is lawful for Christians to accept and execute offices of civil authority when that is their calling.[2] In the administration of such offices they should take care to support true religion, justice, and peace, according to the beneficial laws of each government,[3] and in so doing they may lawfully under the New Testament wage war on just and necessary occasions.[4]

   2. Prv 8.15-16, Rom 13.1-4; see citations under Section 1 above.
   3. Ps 2.10-12, 1 Tm 2.2, Ps 82.3-4, 2 Sm 23.3, 1 Pt 2.13, Ps 101; see citations under Section 1 above.
   4. Lk 3.14, Rom 13.1-4, Mt 8.9-10, Acts 10.1-2, Rv 17.14,16.

# Civil Authorities

3. Civil authorities may not take on themselves the ministering of God's word and the sacraments, the administration of spiritual power, or any interference with matters of faith.[5] Nevertheless it is the duty of civil authorities to protect the church of our Lord, without giving preference to any denomination of Christians, so that every person with church affiliations or duties will be able to function with complete and unquestioned freedom. Since Jesus Christ has directed the establishment of regular government and discipline in his church, no law of any civil government should interfere with, abridge, or hinder the proper exercise of church government among the voluntary members of Christian denominations, acting in accordance with their own professed beliefs. It is the duty of civil authorities to protect the person and good name of all people so that none are abused, injured, or insulted on account of their religious faith or lack of it.[6] It is also their duty to see to it that all religious and ecclesiastical assemblies are held without disturbance.[7]

5. 2 Chr 26.18, Mt 18.17, 16.19, 1 Cor 12.28-29, Eph 4.11-12, 1 Cor 4.1-2, Rom 10.15, Heb 5.4, Jn 18.36, Acts 5.29.
6. Is 49.23, Ps 122.9, Ezr 7.23-28, Lv 24.16, Dt 13.5-6,12, 2 Kgs 18.4, 1 Chr 13.1-9, 2 Kgs 23.1-26, 2 Chr 34.33, 15.12-13, Rom 13.1-6, Ps 105.15, Acts 18.14-16.
7. 2 Chr 19.8-11, 29 and 30, Mt 2.4-5, 2 Sm 23.3, Rom 13.4; see General Note.

## Civil Authorities

4. It is people's duty to pray for those in authority,[8] to honor them,[9] to pay them taxes and whatever is owed them,[10] to obey their lawful commands, and to be subject to them for conscience's sake.[11] Unbelief or different religious views on the part of civil authorities does not mean that they are to be disobeyed by believers, including clergymen,[12] in the legitimate pursuit of their duties.[13] The pope, of course, has no power or jurisdiction over civil authorities or the people under them in secular affairs. The pope never has any right to usurp secular authority, particularly capital punishment in cases of what is judged to be heresy or any other fault.[14]

8. 1 Tm 2.1-3.
9. 1 Pt 2.17.
10. Rom 13.6-7, Mt 22.21.
11. Rom 13.5, Ti 3.1.
12. Rom 13.1, 1 Kgs 2.35, Acts 25.9-11, 2 Pt 2.1,10-11, Jude 8-11.
13. 1 Pt 2.13-14,16; this is an inference from the duties just stated.
14. 2 Thes 2.4, Rv 13.15-17, 2 Tm 2.24, 1 Pt 5.3; this is an inference from the doctrine of the civil magistrate, and from duties incumbent on believers with respect to him.

# Chapter 24
## Marriage and Divorce

1. Marriage is to be between one man and one woman. It is not lawful for any man to have more than one wife, nor for any woman to have more than one husband at the same time.[1]

   1. Gn 2.24, Mt 19.4-6, Prv 2.17, 1 Cor 7.2, Mk 10.6-9, Rom 7.3.

2. Marriage was ordained for the mutual help of husband and wife,[2] for the legitimate propagation of mankind, for raising up a holy seed to the church,[3] and for the prevention of moral impurity.[4]

   2. Gn 2.18.
   3. Mal 2.15, Gn 9.1.
   4. 1 Cor 7.2,9.

3. All people who are mentally, emotionally, and physically capable may legally marry.[5] But it is the duty of Christians to marry only in the Lord. Therefore, those who profess the true reformed religion should not marry infidels, Roman Catholics, or other idolaters. The godly should not be unequally yolked in marriage with any who live a notoriously wicked life or who mantain damnable heresies.[6]

   5. Heb 13.4, 1 Tm 4.3, 1 Cor 7.36-38, Gn 24.57-58.
   6. 1 Cor 7.39, Gn 34.14, Ex 34.16, Dt 7.3-4, 1 Kgs 11.4, Neh 13.25-27, Mal 2.11-12, 2 Cor 6.14.

4. Marriage should not occur where the nearness of blood relationship is forbidden in the Bible.[7] Incestuous marriage can never be legitimized by any human law or consent of the parties involved.[8]

   7. Lv 18, 1 Cor 5.1, Am 2.7.
   8. Mk 6.18, Lv 18.24-28, 20.19-21.

5. If adultery or fornication is discovered after a contractual commitment to marry has been made, but before the marriage itself, the innocent party has the right to dissolve the contract.[9] In the case of adultery after marriage, it is lawful for the innocent party to sue for divorce[10] and after the divorce to marry someone else, as if the guilty party were dead.[11]

    9. Mt 1.18-20, Dt 22.23.
   10. Mt 5.31-32.
   11. Mt 19.9, Rom 7.2-3.

6. Although the corrupt nature of man is inclined to support arguments for the wrong separation of those whom God has joined together in marriage, yet the only causes which warrant dissolving the bond of marriage are adultery or deliberate desertion which cannot be remedied in any way by the church or civil authority.[12] Proceedings for divorce must be public and orderly, and the persons involved must not be allowed to manage their cases according to their own desires and judgment.[13]

   12. Mt 19.6,8-9, 1 Cor 7.15.
   13. Dt 24.1-4, Ezr 10.3.

*The original 1647 Chapter 24 and its 1788 American counterpart had 15 notes. After 1861 PCUS combined notes 6 and 7 as note 6 at the end of paragraph 3. Original note 10 (Lv 20.19-21) disappeared in both PCUS and PCUSA versions along with the passage it supported at the end of paragraph 4 (see Appendix), but PCUS added the citation to the previous note.*

# Chapter 24 (UP)
## Of Marriage and Divorce

1. Christian marriage is an institution ordained of God, blessed by our Lord Jesus Christ, established and sanctified for the happiness and welfare of mankind, into which spiritual and physical union one man and one woman enter, cherishing a mutual esteem and love, bearing with each other's infirmities and weaknesses, comforting each other in trouble, providing in honesty and industry for each other and for their household, praying for each other, and living together the length of their days as heirs of the grace of life.

2. Because the corruption of man is apt unduly to put asunder those whom God has joined together in marriage, and because the church is concerned with the establishment of marriage in the Lord as Scripture sets it forth, and with the present penitence as well as with the past innocence or guilt of those whose marriage has been broken; therefore as a breach of that holy relation may occasion divorce, so remarriage after a divorce granted on grounds explicitly stated in Scripture or implicit in the gospel of Christ may be sanctioned in keeping with his redemptive gospel, when sufficient penitence for sin and failure is evident, and a firm purpose of and endeavor after Christian marriage is manifest.

# Chapter 24 (26, PC)
## Of Marriage and Divorce

1. Marriage is a union between one man and one woman, designed of God to last so long as they both shall live.[1]

   > 1. Gn 2.23-24, 1 Cor 7.2,39, Mt 19.4-6, Eph 5.28,31,33, 1 Cor 13.8,13, Mt 5.31-32, Mk 10.5-9, Rom 7.2-3.

2. Marriage is designed for the mutual help of husband and wife;[2] for the safeguarding, undergirding, and development of their moral and spiritual character;[3] for the propagation of children and the rearing of them in the discipline and instruction of the Lord.[4]

   > 2. Gn 2.18,24.
   > 3. Gn 1.27-28, Eph 5.22-23, Col 3.18-19, Gn 2.18-25, 1 Cor 7.3-5,9,36.
   > 4. Gn 1.27-28, 9.1, Mal 2.15, Mt 18.5-6,10,14, 19.14, Eph 6.1-4, Col 3.20-21, Mk 10.13-16, Lk 18.15-17.

3. All persons who are able with judgment to give their consent may marry,[5] except within the limits of blood relationship forbidden by Scripture,[6] and such marriages are valid before God in the eyes of the church.[7] But no marriage can be fully and securely Christian in spirit or in purpose unless both partners are committed to a common Christian faith and to a deeply shared intention of building a Christian home. Evangelical Christians should seek as partners in marriage only persons who hold in common a sound basis of evangelical faith.[8]

   > 5. Gn 1.27-28.
   > 6. Mk 6.18, 1 Cor 5.1, Lv 18.6-18.
   > 7. Mk 1.30, Jn 2.1-2, 1 Tm 5.14, Heb 13.4, 1 Cor 7.7,36, 9.5, 1 Tm 4.3.
   > 8. 1 Cor 7, esp. v. 39, 2 Cor 6.14-15.

# Of Marriage and Divorce

4. Marriage for the Christian has religious as well as civil significance.[9] The distinctive contribution of the church in performing the marriage ceremony is to affirm the divine institution of marriage;[10] to invoke God's blessing upon those who enter into the marital relationship in accordance with his word;[11] to hear the vows of those who desire to be married; and to assure the married partners of God's grace within their new relationship.[12]

9. Prv 18.22, Mt 19.6, Eph 5.29-30,32, Mk 10.9,11-12.
10. Gn 1.27-28.
11. Mk 10.9.
12. Eph 5.22-23.

5. It is the divine intention that persons entering the marriage covenant become inseparably united, thus allowing for no dissolution save that caused by the death of either husband or wife.[13] However, the weaknesses of one or both partners may lead to gross and persistent denial of the marriage vows so that marriage dies at the heart and the union becomes intolerable; yet only in cases of extreme, unrepented-of, and irremediable unfaithfulness (physical or spiritual) should separation or divorce be considered. Such separation or divorce is accepted as permissible only because of the failure of one or both of the partners, and does not lessen in any way the divine intention for indissoluble union.[14]

13. Gn 2.23-24, Mt 5.31-32, Mk 10.5-9, Rom 7.2-3,
    1 Cor 7.2,10-11,39, Eph 5.28,31,33, Mt 19.4-9,
    1 Cor 13.4-13.
14. Mk 10. 4-9, 1 Cor 7.12-13,15, Mt 19.7-9.

## Of Marriage and Divorce

6. The remarriage of divorced persons may be sanctioned by the church in keeping with the redemptive gospel of Christ, when sufficient penitence for sin and failure is evident, and a firm purpose of and endeavor after Christian marriage is manifested.[15]

> 15. 2 Sm 12.13, Neh 9.17, Ps 32.5, 130.4,
> Mt 12.31a, 21.31-32, Jn 8.3,11, Rom 3.23,
> Gal 6.1, 1 Tm 2.4, Heb 7.25, 1 Jn 1.9, 2.1-2,
> Lk 7.36-50, 15.11-32, Jn 3.16-17, Rom 10.9-10.

7. Divorced persons should give prayerful thought to discover if God's vocation for them is to remain unmarried, since one failure in this realm raises serious questions as to the rightness and wisdom of undertaking another union.[16]

> 16. Mt 5.31-32, 1 Cor 7.10-11,20,32-35, Mk 10.11,
> Lk 16.18.

# Chapter 25
## The Church

1. The catholic or universal church is invisible and consists of all the elect who have been, are, or ever will be gathered into one under Christ, the head. The church is his body and spouse, the fulness of God, who fills all in all.[1]

   1. Eph 1.10,22-23, 5.23,27,32, Col 1.18.

2. The visible church is also catholic or universal under the gospel, i.e., it is not confined to one nation as previously under the Mosaic Law. It consists of all the people in the world who profess the true religion[2] together with their children.[3] The visible church is the kingdom of the Lord Jesus Christ[4] and the house and family of God,[5] outside of which people cannot ordinarily be saved.[6]

   2. 1 Cor 1.2, 12.12-13, Ps 2.8, Rv 7.9, Rom 15.9-12.
   3. 1 Cor 7.14, Acts 2.39, Ez 16.20-21, Rom 11.16, Gn 3.15, 17.7, Gal 3.7,9,14, Rom 4, Mk 10.13-16.
   4. Mt 13.47, Is 9.7, Col 1.13, Mt 13.31, Ps 72.
   5. Eph 2.19, 3.15, Prv 29.18.
   6. Acts 2.47, Mt 28.19, Acts 2.38, 1 Cor 12.13, Mt 26.26-28,10.32-33.

3. In order to gather and perfect God's people in this life until the end of the world Christ has given the ministry, Scriptures, and ordinances of God to this universal visible church, and by his own presence and Spirit he enables the church to function in this way according to his promise.[7]

   7. 1 Cor 12.23, Eph 4.11-13, Mt 28.19-20, Is 59.21.

4. This universal church has been sometimes more and sometimes less visible.[8] Particular churches, which are members of it, are also more or less pure, depending on how the gospel is accepted and taught, how the ordinances of God are administered, and how public worship is performed.[9]

>    8. Rom 11.3-4, Rv 12.6,14, Acts 9.31.
>    9. Rv 2 and 3, 1 Cor 5.6-7, Acts 2.41-42.

5. The purest churches under heaven are subject both to impurity and error.[10] Some churches have so degenerated that they are not churches of Christ, but synagogues of Satan.[11] Nevertheless, there will always be a church on earth to worship God according to his will.[12]

>    10. 1 Cor 5, 13.12, Rv 2 and 3, Mt 13.24-30,47-48,
>        1 Cor 1.2.
>    11. Rv 18.2, Rom 11.18-22, Rv 2.9.
>    12. Mt 16.18, Ps 102.28, Mt 28.19-20, Ps 72,17.

6. There is no other head of the church than the Lord Jesus Christ.[13] In no sense can the pope in Rome be the head of it. Rather, he is that antichrist, the man of sin and son of damnation, who glorifies himself as opposed to Christ and everything related to God.[14]

>    13. Col 1.18, Eph 1.22.
>    14. Mt 23.8-10, 2Thes 2.3-4,8-9, Rev 13.6, 1Pt 5.2-4.

# Chapter 26
## The Fellowship of God's People

1. All believers are united to Jesus Christ, their head, by his Spirit and by faith, and have fellowship with him in his grace, suffering, death, resurrection, and glory.[1] United to one another in love God's people have fellowship in each other's gifts and grace[2] and are obliged to perform those public and private duties which nourish their mutual good, both spiritually and physically.[3]

   > 1. 1 Jn 1.3, Eph 3.16-19, Jn 1.16, Eph 2.5-6, Phil 3.10, Rom 6.5-6, 2 Tm 2.12, Rom 8.17.
   > 2. Eph 4.15-16, 1 Cor 12.7, 3.21-23, Col 2.19, 1 Jn 1.3,7.
   > 3. 1 Thes 5.11,14, Rom 1.11-12,14, 1 Jn 3.16-18, Gal 6.10.

2. By their profession of faith believers are bound to maintain a holy fellowship and communion with each other in the worship of God and in the performance of other spiritual services for their mutual improvement.[4] They are also bound to help each other in material things according to their different abilities and needs. This fellowship is to be offered, as God gives the opportunity, to everyone in every place who calls on the name of the Lord Jesus.[5]

   > 4. Heb 10.24-25, Acts 2.42,46, Is 2.3, 1 Cor 11.20.
   > 5. Acts 2.44-45, 1 Jn 3.17, 2 Cor 8 and 9, Acts 11.29-30.

## The Fellowship of God's People

3. This communion that God's people have with Christ in no way means that they share in his godhead or are equal with him in any respect—to affirm either is impious and blasphemous.[6] Neither does their communion with each other take away or infringe the right each person has to own and possess goods and property.[7]

> 6. Col 1.18-19, 1 Cor 8.6, Is 42.8, 1 Tm 6.15-16, Ps 45.7, Heb 1.8-9, Ps 14.7.
> 7. Ex 20.15, Eph 4.28, Acts 5.4.

# Chapter 27
## The Sacraments

1. Sacraments are holy signs and seals of the covenant of grace. They were instituted by God along with that covenant[1] to represent Christ and his benefits, to confirm our position with and in him,[2] to demonstrate a visible difference between those who belong to the church and the rest of the world,[3] and solemnly to engage believers in the service of God in Christ according to his word.[4]

    1. Rom 4.11, Gn 17.7,9-11, Mt 28.19, 1 Cor 11.23, Ex 13.9-10, 12.3-20.
    2. 1 Cor 10.16, 11.25-26, Gal 3.27.
    3. Rom 15.8, Ex 12.48, Gn 34.14, 1 Cor 10.21, Heb 13.10, 1 Cor 11.27-29.
    4. Rom 6.3-4, 1 Cor 10.2,14-16,21; see context.

2. In every sacrament there is a spiritual relationship or sacramental union between the sign and the thing signified. And so the names and effects of the one are attributed to the other.[5]

    5. Gn 17.10, Mt 26.27-28, Ti 3.5.

3. The grace revealed in or by the sacraments in their right use does not come from any power in them. Neither does the effectiveness of a sacrament depend on the devoutness or the intention of whoever administers it. Rather the power and effectiveness of the sacraments are the result of the work of the Spirit[6] and rest on God's word instituting them, since his word authorizes their use and promises benefits to worthy receivers of them.[7]

    6. Rom 2.28-29, 1 Pt 3.21, Mt 3.11, 1 Cor 12.13, 3.7, 6.11, Jn 3.5, Acts 8.13-23.
    7. Mt 26.27-28, 28.19-20, Jn 6.63, Lk 22.19-20, 1 Cor 11.26.

4. There are only two sacraments ordained by Christ our Lord in the gospel: baptism and the Lord's supper.[8] Neither of these may be administered by anyone but a lawfully ordained minister of the word.[9]

   8. Mt 28.19, 1 Cor 11.20,23, 4.1, Heb 5.4.
   9. See General Note.

5. The sacraments of the Old Testament signify and reveal in substance the same spiritual things as those of the New.[10]

   10. 1 Cor 10.1-4, 5.7-8, Col 2.11-12.

# Chapter 28
## Baptism

1. Baptism is a sacrament of the New Testament, ordained by Jesus Christ.[1] By baptism a person is solemnly admitted into the visible church.[2] Baptism is also a sign and seal of the covenant of grace,[3] of ingrafting into Christ,[4] of rebirth,[5] of remission of sins,[6] and of yielding to God through Jesus Christ to walk in newness of life.[7] By Christ's own direction this sacrament is to be continued in his church until the end of the world.[8]

   1. Mt 28.19, Mk 16.16.
   2. 1 Cor 12.13, Gal 3.27-28, Acts 2.41, 10.47.
   3. Rom 4.11, Col 2.11-12, Gal 3.29.
   4. Gal 3.27, Rom 6.3-5.
   5. Ti 3.5.
   6. Mk 1.4, Acts 2.38, 22.16.
   7. Rom 6.3-4.
   8. Mt 28.19-20.

2. The physical substance to be used in this sacrament is water. The person is to be baptized in the name of the Father, the Son, and the Holy Spirit[9] by a lawfully called minister of the gospel.[10]

   9. Mt 3.11, Jn 1.33, Mt 28.19-20, Acts 8.36,38, 10.47, Eph 4.11-13.
   10. See General Note.

3. Dipping the person into the water is not necessary. Baptism is correctly administered by pouring or sprinkling water on the person.[11]

   11. Heb 9.10,19-22, Acts 2.41, 16.33, Mk 7.4, Acts 1.5, 2.3-4,17, 11.15-16, 10.46-47, 1 Cor 10.2.

## Baptism

4. Not only those who actually profess faith in and obedience to Christ are to be baptized[12] but also the infants of one or both believing parents.[13]

> 12. Mk 16.15-16, Acts 8.37-38; see citations under Section 1 above, Acts 9.18.
> 13. Gn 17.7,9-10, Gal 3.9,14, Col 2.11-12, Acts 2.38-39, Rom 4.11-12, 1 Cor 7.14, Mt 28.19, Mk 10.13-16, Lk 18.15-16, Acts 16.14-15,33.

5. Although it is a great sin to condemn or neglect this sacrament,[14] baptism is not inseparably connected with God's grace and salvation. One can be saved and reborn without baptism,[15] and, on the other hand, everyone who is baptized is not therefore unquestionably reborn.[16]

> 14. Lk 7.30, Ex 4.24-26, Gn 17.14, Dt 28.9.
> 15. Rom 4.11, Acts 10.2,4,22,31,45-47, Lk 23.40-43.
> 16. Acts 8.13,23.

6. The effectiveness of baptism is not tied to that moment in time in which it is administered.[17] However, by the correct use of this sacrament the grace promised in it is not only offered but actually embodied and conferred by the Holy Spirit to everyone (adult or infant) to whom that grace is given, according to the purpose of God's own will and in his appointed time.[18]

> 17. Jn 3.5,8, Rom 4.11.
> 18. Gal 3.27, Ti 3.5, Eph 5.25-26, Acts 2.38-41, Eph 1.4-5, Acts 16.31,33.

7. The sacrament of baptism should be administered only once to a person.[19]

> 19. Ti 3.5; there is no command, and no adequate example for the repetition of baptism.

# Chapter 29
## The Lord's Supper

1. The night Jesus was betrayed he instituted the sacrament of his body and blood, called the Lord's supper, to be observed in his church until the end of the world as a perpetual remembrance of his sacrifice in death and as the seal of all the benefits of that sacrifice for true believers. It also signifies the spiritual nourishment and growth of believers in Jesus and their additional commitment to perform all the duties they owe him. Finally it is a bond and pledge of believers' communion with Jesus and with each other as members of his mystical body.[1]

   1. 1 Cor 11.23-26, 10.16-17,21, 12.13, Mt 26.26-27, Lk 22.19-20.

2. In this sacrament Christ is not offered up to his Father, nor is any actual sacrifice made for the remission of sins of the living or the dead.[2] Rather, this sacrament commemorates Christ's offering up of himself, by himself, on the cross once for all, and it spiritually offers up to God every possible praise for that sacrifice.[3] Consequently the so-called sacrifice of the Roman Catholic mass does detestable injustice to Christ's one sacrifice, which is the only propitiation for all the sins of the elect.[4]

   2. Heb 9.22,25-26,28.
   3. 1 Cor 11.24-26, Mt 26.26-27, Lk 22.19-20.
   4. Heb 7.23-24,27, 10.11-12,14,18.

# The Lord's Supper

3. In the administration of the Lord's supper Jesus has directed his ministers to declare to the congregation his words instituting this sacrament, to pray, and to bless the bread and wine, which are thus set apart from their ordinary use and put to holy use. His ministers are to take and break the bread, to take the cup, and (communicating themselves, as well) to give both to the communicants—but not to anyone else not present at that time in the congregation.[5]

> 5. Mt 26.26-28, Mk 14.22-24, Lk 22.19-20,
>    1 Cor 11.23-27; see citations under Sections 1 and 2,
>    Acts 20.7, 1 Cor 11.20.

4. Practices contrary to the nature of this sacrament and to the institution of it by Christ are private masses or receiving the sacrament alone from a priest or anyone else;[6] denying the cup to the congregation;[7] and worshiping the bread and wine themselves by lifting them up or carrying them around for adoration or reserving them for any counterfeit religious use.[8]

> 6. 1 Cor 10.6, 1 Tm 1.3-4.
> 7. Mk 4.23, 1 Cor 11.25-29.
> 8. Mt 15.9; there is not the least appearance of a
>    warrant for any of these things, either in precept or
>    example, in any part of the word of God; see all the
>    places in which the ordinance is mentioned.

5. The bread and wine in this sacrament, properly set apart to the uses ordained by Christ, so relate to him crucified that truly and yet only sacramentally they are sometimes called by the name of what they represent, that is, the body and blood of Christ.[9] Even so, they still remain in substance and nature only bread and wine, as they were before their sacramental use.[10]

> 9. Mt 26.26-28.
> 10. 1 Cor 11.26-28, Mt 26.29.

6. The teaching that the substance of the bread and wine is changed into the substance of Christ's body and blood (usually called transubstantiation) by the consecration of a priest or any other means is objectionable not only to Scripture but even to common sense and reason. Such teaching overturns the nature of the sacrament and has been and is the cause of much superstition and indeed flagrant idolatry.[11]

> 11. Acts 3.21, 1 Cor 11.24-26, Lk 24.6,39; these statements are inferences from the doctrine of the sacraments and do not require specific Scripture proofs.

7. Worthy receivers, physically partaking of the visible substances of this sacrament, do then also by faith actually and in fact, but not physically or bodily, spiritually receive and feed on Christ crucified and on all the benefits of his death. The body and blood of Christ are not then bodily or physically in, with, or under the bread and wine; but they are actually spiritually present to the faith of believers in the administration of this sacrament, just as the bread and wine are physically present.[12]

> 12. 1 Cor 11.28, 5.7-8, 10.16,3-4, Jn 6.53,58; see note under Section 6 above.

# The Lord's Supper

8. Although ignorant or wicked men may partake of the physical substances in this sacrament, they do not receive what is signified by them. However, by their unworthy coming to the Lord's table they are guilty of his body and blood and bring condemnation on themselves. Therefore, just as the ignorant and ungodly are not fit to enjoy communion with Christ, neither are they worthy to come to the Lord's table, and, as long as they remain ignorant and ungodly, they cannot and must not be allowed to partake of the holy mystery of communion without committing a great sin against Christ.[13]

13. 1 Cor 11.27-29, 2 Cor 6.14-16, 1 Cor 10.21, 5.6-7,13,
2 Thes 3.6,14-15, Mt 7.6.

# Chapter 30
## Condemnation by the Church

1. As king and head of his church, the Lord Jesus has directed the establishment of church government, separate from civil authority, which is to be administered by officers of the church.[1]

    1. Is 9.6-7, 1 Tm 5.17, 1 Thes 5.12, Acts 20.17,28, Heb 13.7,17,24, 1 Cor 12.28, Mt 28.18-20, Ps 2.6-9, Jn 18.36.

2. To these officers are committed the keys of the kingdom of heaven, which empower them: to free people from the guilt of sin or to bind them to it; to close the kingdom of heaven to the unrepentant by the word and condemnation; and to open the kingdom to repentant sinners by the ministry of the gospel and by withdrawing condemnation as the occasion demands.[2]

    2. Mt 16.19, 18.17-18, Jn 20.21-23, 2 Cor 2.6-8.

3. Condemnation by the church is necessary in order to reclaim and regain spiritual brothers who have committed some serious offense; to deter others from committing similar offenses; to purge that leaven which might contaminate the whole lump; to vindicate the honor of Christ and the holy profession of the gospel; and to avoid the wrath of God, which might justly fall on the church, should it allow his covenant and the sacraments to be profaned by notorious and obstinate offenders.[3]

    3. 1 Cor 5, 1 Tm 5.20, Mt 7.6, 1 Tm 1.20, 1 Cor 11.27-34, Jude 23, 2 Sm 12.14.

## Condemnation by the Church

4. The best way to accomplish these purposes is for the officers of the church to act in accordance with the severity of the offense and the guilt of the offender by warning the offender, excluding him from the sacrament of the Lord's supper for a time, or excommunicating him from the church.[4]

> 4. 1 Thes 5.12, 2 Thes 3.6,14-15, 1 Cor 5.4-5,13, Mt 18.17, Ti 3.10.

# Chapter 31
## Synods and Councils

1. The assemblies which are generally called synods or councils ought to be held for the better government and continuing improvement of the church. By virtue of their office and the power Christ has given them to build up and not destroy, the leaders of particular churches should arrange for such assemblies and meet together in them as often as is judged necessary for the good of the church.[1]

> 1. Acts 15.1-41, Rv 2.1-6, Acts 20.17,28, Is 49.23,
> 1 Tm 2.1-2, 2 Chr 19.8-11, 29-30, Mt 2.4-5, Prv 11.14,
> Acts 15, 20.17.

2. As far as the ministry is concerned, it is the responsibility of synods and councils to settle controversies of faith and cases relating to matters of conscience, to set down rules and directions for the better administration of the public worship of God and of church government, and to hear complaints in cases of maladministration and authoritatively to settle them. If these decisions conform to the word of God, they are to be accepted reverently and submissively, not only because they agree with the word but also because they rest on authority ordained and arranged by God in his word.[2]

> 2. Acts 15.15,19,24,27-31, 16.4, Mt 18.17-20,29.

3. Since apostolic times all synods and councils, whether general or local, may make mistakes, and many have. Consequently synods and councils are not to be made a final authority in questions of faith and living but are to be used as an aid to both.[3]

> 3. Eph 2.20, Acts 17.11, 1 Cor 2.5, 2 Cor 1.24; see
> General Note.

## *Synods andCouncils*

4. Synods and councils should consider and settle only ecclesiastical questions. They are not to meddle in civil affairs which concern the state except in extraordinary cases of modest petitions or in an advisory capacity prompted by religious conscience, when requested by civil authorities.[4]

> 4. Lk 12.13-14, Jn 18.36, Mt 22.21.

# Chapter 32
## The Condition of Man after Death and the Resurrection of the Dead

1. After death the bodies of human beings decompose and return to dust,[1] but their souls, which do not die or sleep, have an immortal existence and immediately return to God who created them.[2] The souls of the righteous are then perfected in holiness and are received into the highest heavens, where they behold the face of God in light and glory and wait for the full redemption of their bodies.[3] The souls of the wicked are thrown into hell, where they remain in torment and complete darkness, set apart for the great day of judgment.[4] Scripture recognizes only these two places, and no other, for souls separated from their bodies.

> 1. Gn 3.19, Acts 13.36.
> 2. Lk 23.43, Eccl 12.7, Phil 1.23, 2 Cor 5.6-8.
> 3. Heb 12.23, 2 Cor 5.1,6,8, Phil 1.23, Acts 3.21,
>    Eph 4.10, 1 Jn 3.2, Lk 16.23, Rom 8.23; see under
>    figure 2 above, Rv 7.4,15.
> 4. Lk 16.23-24, Acts 1.25, Jude 6-7, 1 Pt 3.19, 2 Pt 2.9.

2. Those who are alive at the last day will not die but will be changed.[5] At that time all the dead will be raised with the very same bodies and no other than the same bodies they had before, although with different characteristics, which will be united again to their souls forever.[6]

> 5. 1 Thes 4.17, 1 Cor 15.51-52.
> 6. Jb 19.26-27, 1 Cor 15.42-44; see preceding context.

### The Condition of Man after Death and the Resurrection of the Dead

3. By the power of Christ the bodies of the unjust shall be raised to dishonor, but by his Spirit the bodies of the just will be raised to honor and be made according to the pattern of his own glorious body.[7]

> 7. Acts 24.15, Jn 5.28-29, 1 Cor 15.42, Phil 3.21.

# Chapter 33
## The Last Judgment

1. God the Father has ordained a day in which he will judge the world in righteousness by Jesus Christ,[1] to whom he has given all power and judgment.[2] In that day not only will the apostate angels be judged, but all the people who have lived on earth will appear before the court of Christ to give an account of their thoughts, words, and actions, and be judged according to what they have done in the body, whether good or evil.[3]

   1. Acts 17.31, Mt 25.31-34.
   2. Jn 5.22,27.
   3. 1 Cor 6.3, Jude 6, 2 Pt 2.4, 2 Cor 5.10, Eccl 12.14, Rom 2.16, 14.10,12, Mt 12.36-37, 1 Cor 3.13-15.

2. God's purpose in arranging for this day is to show forth the glory of his mercy in the eternal salvation of the his chosen people[4] and the glory of his justice in the damnation of the reprobate, who are wicked and disobedient.[5] At that time the righteous will go into everlasting life and receive that fulness of joy and refreshment which will come from the presence of the Lord.[6] But the wicked, who do not know God and do not obey the gospel of Jesus Christ, will be thrown into eternal torment and punished with everlasting destruction away from the presence of the Lord and the glory of his power.[7]

   4. Rom 9.23, Mt 25.21, Eph 2.4-7.
   5. Rom 2.5-6, 2 Thes 1.7-8, Rom 9.22.
   6. Mt 25.31-34, Acts 3.19, 2 Thes 1.7, Ps 16.11.
   7. Mt 25.41,46, 2 Thes 1.9, Is 66.24, Mk 9.47-48.

# The Last Judgement

3. Christ wants us to be completely convinced that there is going to be a day of judgment, as a deterrent to sin for everyone and as an added consolation for the godly in their suffering.[8] He has also made sure that no one knows when that day will be, so that we may never rest secure in our worldly surroundings, but, not knowing what hour the Lord will come, we must always be alert and may always be ready to say, "Come, Lord Jesus, come quickly."[9] Amen.

8. 2 Pt 3.11,14, 2 Cor 5.10-11, 2 Thes 1.5-7, Lk 21.27-28, Rom 8.23-25.
9. Mt 24.36,42-44, Mk 13.35-37, Lk 12.35-36, Rv 22.20.

# Chapter 34
## The Holy Spirit

1. The Holy Spirit, the third person in the Trinity, proceeding from the Father and the Son, of the same substance and equal in power and glory, is, together with the Father and the Son, to be believed in, loved, obeyed, and worshiped throughout all ages.

> 2 Cor 13.14, Jn 15.26, Mt 28.19, 3.16-17, Lk 1.35,
> Eph 4.30, Heb 10.29, 1 Cor 10.10-11, Rv 22.17,
> Eph 2.18-20,22, Jn 14.26, 16.7, Gal 4.4-6,
> Acts 5.3-4, 16.6-7, Mk 3.29, Rom 8.26-27, 1 Jn 2.20-27,
> Acts 2.33, Jn 20.22, Rom 8.14, 1 Thes 5.19, Jn 4.24.

2. He is the Lord and giver of life, everywhere present, and is the source of all good thoughts, pure desires, and holy counsels in men. By him the prophets were moved to speak the word of God, and all the writers of the Holy Scriptures inspired to record infallibly the mind and will of God. The dispensation of the gospel is especially committed to him. He prepares the way for it, accompanies it with his persuasive power, and urges its message upon the reason and conscience of men, so that they who reject its merciful offer are not only without excuse, but are also guilty of resisting the Holy Spirit.

> Eph 4.30, 5.9, Gn 1.2, Jn 3.5,7, Acts 2.1-21, Gal 5.22-25,
> Jn 16.8-11, 2 Pt 1.21, 2 Tm 3.16, 1 Cor 2.9-10,13,
> 1 Pt 1.11, Jn 16.13-15, Acts 7.51, 1 Thes 5.19,
> Ps 104.30, 139.7, Acts 28.25, 1.8, 2.7, Rom 8.9,14-16,
> Ti 3.5-6, Rom 5.5, Mt 12.31-32.

# The Holy Spirit

3. The Holy Spirit, whom the Father is ever willing to give to all who ask him, is the only efficient agent in the application of redemption. He regenerates men by his grace, convicts them of sin, moves them to repentance, and persuades and enables them to embrace Jesus Christ by faith. He unites all believers to Christ, dwells in them as their comforter and sanctifier, gives to them the spirit of adoption and prayer, and performs all these gracious offices by which they are sanctified and sealed unto the day of redemption.

> Jn 3.1-8, Acts 2.38, Lk 11.13, 1 Cor 12.3,
> Jn 7.37-39, 16.13, 16.7-11, Rv 22.17, Ti 3.5-7,
> 2 Thes 2.13, Gal 4.6, 1 Jn 4.2, Rom 8.14-17,26-27,
> Eph 4.30, 1 Cor 2.13-14, Eph 1.13, 1 Thes 1.5, Gal 6.8,
> Eph 2.18, 5.9, 4.3, Jude 20-21, Rom 15.16,
> Heb 10.14-15, 1 Cor 6.19, 3.16.

4. By the indwelling of the Holy Spirit all believers being vitally united to Christ, who is the head, are thus united one to another in the church, which is his body. He calls and anoints ministers for their holy office, qualifies all other officers in the church for their special work, and imparts various gifts and graces to its members. He gives efficacy to the word and to the ordinances of the gospel. By him the church will be preserved, increased, purified, and at last made perfectly holy in the presence of God.

> Eph 2.14-18, 4.1-6,30, 5.18, Acts 2.4, 13.2-3,
> 1 Cor 12.4-13, 2 Pt 1.19-21, 1 Thes 1.5-6, Jn 20.22-23,
> Mt 28.19-20, Acts 20.28, 6.3,5-6, Gal 5.16,22-23,
> 2 Tm 3.16, Jn 16.13-14, 1 Cor 2.10, Rv 2.7,
> Acts 1.8, Rv 22.17.

# Chapter 35
## The Gospel of the Love of God and Missions

1. God in infinite and perfect love, having provided in the covenant of grace, through the mediation and sacrifice of the Lord Jesus Christ, a way of life and salvation, sufficient for and adapted to the whole lost race of man, freely offers this salvation to all men in the gospel.

> Rv 22.17, Jn 3.16, 1 Jn 2.1-2, Acts 2.38-39,
> Mt 11.28-30, 2 Cor 5.14-19, Ti 2.11, Heb 2.9,
> Lk 24.46-47, Jer 31.3, 1 Jn 4.9,16, Ti 3.4-5.
> Heb 13.20-21, 12.22-24, 8.10, Eph 2.8, 1 Tm 2.5-6,
> Heb 9.26, 1 Cor 15.3, Rom 5.6,8,
> Jn 10.10-11, 11.25, 14.6,19, Phil 1.21, Acts 4.12,
> Rom 1.16, Heb 5.9, 2 Pt 3.9, Mt 24.14, Jn 4.42,
> Rv 11.15, Rom 6.23, 2 Cor 9.15.

2. In the gospel God declares his love for the world and his desire that all men should be saved; reveals fully and clearly the only way of salvation; promises eternal life to all who truly repent and believe in Christ; invites and commands all to embrace the offered mercy; and by his Spirit accompanying the word pleads with men to accept his gracious invitation.

> Mt 28.19-20, Acts 4.12, Jn 6.37-40, 17.3,
> Acts 16.30-31, 2.38, Gal 2.16-20, Rom 1.16-17, 4.5,
> Acts 13.38-39,48, 2 Pt 3.9, Mt 11.28-30, Mk 1.14-15,
> Acts 17.30, Rv 22.17, Ez 33.11, Is 1.18, Lk 13.34,
> Jn 3.16-17, 1 Jn 4.9-10, Is 45.22, Heb 10.19-22, Jn 14.6,
> Rom 10.9, 1 Pt 1.8-9, Heb 3.7-8, 2 Cor 6.2, Heb 4.16,
> Rom 5.8, 2 Thes 3.5, Phil 2.12-13, Jn 16.13-14.

# The Gospel of the Love of God and Missions

3. It is the duty and privilege of everyone who hears the gospel immediately to accept its merciful provisions; and they who continue in impenitence and unbelief incur aggravated guilt and perish by their own fault.

> Heb 2.3, 12.25, Acts 13.46, Mt 10.32-33, Lk 12.47-48,
> Heb 10.29, 1 Thes 5.9-10, Jn 1.12, Heb 4.16, Rv 22.17,
> 1 Tm 6.12, Jn 3.18, Mt 25.46, Rom 6.23.

4. Since there is no other way of salvation than that revealed in the gospel, and since in the divinely established and ordinary method of grace faith comes by hearing the word of God, Christ has commissioned his church to go into all the world and to make disciples of all nations. All believers are, therefore, under obligation to sustain the ordinances of the Christian religion where they are already established, and to contribute by their prayers, gifts, and personal efforts to the extension of the kingdom of Christ throughout the whole earth.

> Acts 4.12, Mt 28.19-20, Acts 1.8, Rom 10.13-17,
> Heb 10.19-25, Gal 3.28, 1 Cor 16.1-2, Mt 9.36-38,
> Acts 13.2-4, Col 3.16, Rv 22.17, Col 1.28-29, Acts 16.31,
> 2 Tm 3.15, Jn 5.39, Mt 24.14, 13.38, Jn 17.18,
> Acts 20.28, 1 Pt 5.2, Jn 21.15-16, 1 Cor 3.9, 11.24,
> 2 Cor 1.11, Eph 6.18-19, Heb 13.16, Gal 6.6,
> Mt 10.8, 2 Cor 9.7, 2 Tm 2.15, Rom 12.11, Col 3.23-24,
> Mt 6.10,13, Rv 11.15.

# Appendix
## Changes to the Text

Listed below are all the variations in the text prior to the 1902 American version and subsequent to it. In this list the different editions and versions are identified as follows: 1647— the original English edition; AM — the American edition up through 1902 that we have modernized; UP — the version as revised by the PCUSA and UPCUSA; PC — the version as revised by the PCUS; and ARP — the version as revised by the Associate Reformed Presbyterian Church.

Our reference text for the 1647 edition has been the copy in Philip Schaff, ed., *The Creeds of Christendom*, 4th ed. (New York: Harper, 1919), 3:600-673. For AM we have used the notes to Schaff, the PCUS edition of 1910 (which contains the 1910 changes to the proof texts), the PCUSA text of 1896, and the American edition of 1839. For UP we have referred to the UPCUSA *Book of Confessions*, 2nd ed. (New York, 1970), reading them against the UPCUSA and PCUSA editions printed in 1969, 1958, 1953, and 1924. The last change to the PCUS text was proposed in 1962 and adopted in 1963; consequently for PC we have used their 1963 edition. The ARPs have made minor changes to the *Confession* as late as 2001. We have referred to their latest edition (2000) and its addenda.

Variant readings are listed below by chapter and section with the AM reading first followed by a semicolon and the other readings.

(1.title) Scripture] AM, 1647, UP, PC; Scriptures ARP

(1.1) inexcusable; yet are they] AM, UP, PC; inexcusable; yet they are ARP; unexcusable; yet are they 1647

(1.2) The Revelation] AM. UP, ARP; The Revelation of John 1647; Revelation PC

(1.5) esteem for the Holy Scripture] AM, PC; esteem of the Holy Scripture 1647, UP, ARP

## Changes to the Text

(1.6) and that there are] AM, PC, ARP; and there are 1647, UP

(1.8) into the vulgar language of every nation] AM, 1647, UP, ARP; into the language of every people PC

(1.9) it may be searched] AM, UP, PC; it must be searched 1647, ARP


(2.2) nor deriving ] AM, 1647, UP, PC; not deriving ARP


(3.title) Of God's Eternal Decrees] AM, PC; Of God's Eternal Decree 1647, UP, ARP

(3.5) of his mere free grace and love] AM, 1647, ARP; of his free grace and love alone UP, PC


(5.5) support upon himself] AM, UP, PC, ARP; support unto himself 1647


(7.3) wherein he freely offereth] AM, 1647, UP; wherein he freely offered PC; whereby he freely offereth ARP


(9.1) that it is neither] AM, UP, PC, ARP; that is neither 1647

(9.2) which is good] AM, UP, PC, ARP; which was good 1647

(9.5) to good alone] AM, 1647, UP, PC; to do good alone ARP


(10.1) and those only] AM, 1647, UP, PC; and them only ARP

(10.4) come to Christ] AM, 1647, UP, PC; come unto Christ ARP

(10.4) and maintain that they may is very pernicious, and to be detested] AM, 1647, ARP; and maintain that they may is without warrant of the word of God UP, PC

## Changes to the Text

(11.1) not by imputing] AM, UP, PC, ARP; nor by imputing 1647


(16.4) requires, that] AM, UP, PC; requires, as that 1647, ARP

(16.5) because of the great] AM, 1647, UP, PC; by reason of the great ARP

(16.7) Works done by unregenerate men, although for the matter of them they may be things which God commands, and of good use both to themselves and others; yet because they proceed not from a heart purified by faith; nor are done in a right manner, according to the word; nor to a right end, the glory of God; they are therefore sinful, and cannot please God, or make a man meet to receive grace from God. And yet their neglect of them is more sinful, and displeasing unto God] AM, 1647, PC, ARP; Works done by unregenerate men, although for the matter of them they may be things which God commands, and in themselves praiseworthy and useful, and although the neglect of such things is sinful and displeasing unto God; yet, because they proceed not from a heart purified by faith; nor are done in a right manner, according to his Word; nor to a right end, the glory of God; they come short of what God requires, and do not make any man meet to receive the grace of God UP


(18.1) in a state of grace] AM, 1647, UP, PC; in the state of grace ARP


(20.1) and a willing mind] AM, UP, PC; and willing mind 1647, ARP

(20.1) fuller communications] AM, PC, ARP; full communications 1647, UP

(20.2) commandments] AM, UP, PC, ARP; commands 1647

(20.2) the requiring an] AM, PC; the requiring of 1647, UP, ARP

(20.4) powers which God] AM, UP, PC, ARP; power which God 1647

(20.4) censures of the church] AM, UP, PC; censures of the church, and by the power of the civil magistrate 1647; censures of the church; and in proportion as their erroneous opinions or practices, either in their own nature or in the manner of publishing or maintaining them, are destructive to the external peace of the church and of civil society, they may also be proceeded against by the power of the civil magistrate ARP

(21.1) limited by] AM, UP, PC, ARP; limited to 1647

(21.1) representation] AM, UP, PC, ARP; representations 1647

(21.4) not for the dead, nor for those of whom it may be known that they have sinned the sin unto death] AM, 1647, ARP; not for the dead UP, PC

(21.5) oaths, and vows] AM, UP, PC, ARP; oaths, vows 1647

(21.5) special occasions] AM, UP, ARP; several occasions 1647; special occasion PC

(21.6) spirit and in truth] AM, UP, PC, ARP; spirit and truth 1647

(22.3) perform. Yet it is a sin to refuse an oath touching anything that is good and just, being imposed by lawful authority] AM, 1647, PC, ARP; perform UP

(22.6) for obtaining] AM, UP, PC; for the obtaining 1647, ARP

(22.7) in his own power] AM, 1647, UP, PC; in his power ARP

(22.7) which respects, Popish monastical] AM, ARP; which respect, popish monastical 1647; which respects, monastical UP, PC

## Changes to the Text

(23.2) just and necessary occasions] AM, UP, PC, ARP; just and necessary occasion 1647

(23.3) Civil magistrates may not assume to themselves the administration of the word and sacraments; or the power of the keys of the kingdom of heaven; or, in the least, interfere in matters of faith. Yet, as nursing fathers, it is the duty of civil magistrates to protect the church of our common Lord, without giving the preference to any denomination of Christians above the rest, in such a manner that all ecclesiastical persons whatever shall enjoy the full, free, and unquestioned liberty of discharging every part of their sacred functions, without violence or danger. And, as Jesus Christ hath appointed a regular government and discipline in his church, no law of any commonwealth should interfere with, let, or hinder, the due exercise thereof, among the voluntary members of any denomination of Christians, according to their own profession and belief. It is the duty of civil magistrates to protect the person and good name of all their people, in such an effectual manner as that no person be suffered, either upon pretense of religion or infidelity, to offer any indignity, violence, abuse, or injury to any other person whatsoever; and to take order, that all religious and ecclesiastical assemblies be held without molestation or disturbance] AM, UP, PC; The civil magistrate may not assume to himself the administration of the Word and Sacraments, or the power of the keys of the kingdom of heaven: yet he hath authority, and it is his duty to take order, that unity and peace be preserved in the Church, that the truth of God be kept pure and entire, that all blasphemies and heresies be suppressed, all corruptions and abuses in worship and discipline prevented or reformed, and all ordinances of God duly settled, administered, and observed. For the better effecting whereof he hath power to call synods, to be present at them, and to provide that whatsoever is transacted in them be according to the mind of God 1647; The civil magistrate may not assume to himself administration of the word and sacraments, or the power of the keys of the kingdom of heaven; yet, as the gospel revelation lays indispensable obligations upon all classes of people who are favored with it, magistrates as such, are bound to execute their respective offices in a subserviency thereunto, administering government on Christian principles, and ruling in the fear of God, according to the directions of his word, as those who shall give an account to the Lord Jesus, whom God hath appointed to be the judge of the world. Hence, magistrates, as such, in a Christian country, are bound to promote the Christian religion, as the most valuable interest of their subjects, by all such means as are not inconsistent with civil rights; and do not imply an interference with the policy of the church, which is the free and independent kingdom of the Redeemer; nor an assumption of dominion over conscience ARP

(24.3) infidels, papists, or other idolaters] AM, 1647, UP, PC; infidels or other idolaters ARP

(24.4) as man and wife] UP and PC *before 1903 and subsequent twentieth-century revisions*; as man and wife. The man may not marry any of his wife's kindred nearer in blood than he may of his own, nor the woman of her husband's kindred nearer in blood than of her own 1647, AM *before the split into PCUSA and PCUS*, ARP

(25.2) together with their children] AM, UP, PC, ARP; and of their children 1647

(25.2) out of which there is no ordinary possibility of salvation] AM, 1647, ARP; through which men are ordinarily saved, and union with which is essential to their best growth and service UP, PC

## Changes to the Text

(25.5) as to become no churches of Christ, but synagogues of Satan] AM, 1647, ARP; as to become apparently no churches of Christ UP, PC

(25.6) There is no other head of the Chruch but the Lord Jesus Christ: nor can the Pope of Rome, in any sense be head thereof; but is that Antichrist, that man of sin and son of perdition, that exalteth himself in the Church against Christ, and all that is called God] AM, 1647; The Lord Jesus Christ is the only head of the Church, and the claim of any man to be the vicar of Christ and the head of the Church is unscriptural, without warrant in fact, and is a usurpation dishonoring to the Lord Jesus Christ UP; The Lord Jesus Christ is the only head of the church, and the claim of any man to be the vicar of Christ and the head of the church, is without warrant in fact or in Scripture, even anti-Christian, a usurpation dishonoring to the Lord Jesus Christ PC; There is no other head of the church but the Lord Jesus Christ; nor can mere man in any sense be the head thereof ARP

(26.1) All saints that are united] AM, 1647, UP, ARP; All saints being united PC

(26.2) saints by profession] AM, 1647, UP, ARP; saints by their profession PC

(26.3) property] AM, UP, PC, ARP; propriety 1647

(27.2) and effects] AM, UP, PC, ARP; and the effects 1647

(29.2) but only a commemoration of that one offering up of himself, by himself, upon the cross, once for all, and a spiritual oblation of all possible praise unto God for the same; so that the popish sacrifice of the mass, as they call it, is most abominably injurious to Christ's one only sacrifice, the alone propitiation for all the sins of the elect] AM, 1647, ARP; but a commemoration of that one offering up of himself, by himself, upon the cross, once for all, and a spiritual oblation of all possible praise unto God for the same; so that the so-called sacrifice of the mass is most contradictory to Christ's one sacrifice, the only propitiation for all the sins of the elect UP, PC

(29.3) to give both to the communicants but to none who are not then present in the congregation] AM, 1647, UP, ARP; to give both to the communicants PC

(29.8) body and blood of the Lord, to their own damnation. Wherefore all ignorant and ungodly persons, as they are unfit to enjoy communion with him, so are they unworthy of the Lord's table, and cannot, without great sin against Christ, while they remain such, partake of these holy mysteries, or be admitted thereunto] AM, 1647, ARP; body and blood of the Lord, and bring judgment on themselves. Wherefore all ignorant and ungoldly persons, as they are unfit to enjoy communion with him, so are they unworthy of the Lord's Table, and cannot, without great sin against Christ, while they remain such, partake of these holy mysteries, or be admitted thereunto UP; body and blood of the Lord, and bring judgment on themselves PC

(30.3) from like offenses] AM, UP, PC; from the like offenses 1647, ARP

(31.1) commonly called synods or councils: and it belongeth to the overseers and other rulers of the particular churches, by virtue of their office, and the power which Christ hath given them for edification, and not for destruction, to appoint such assemblies; and to convene together in them, as often as they shall judge it expedient for the good of the church] AM, UP, PC; commonly called synods or councils 1647, ARP

# Changes to the Text

(31.2) *This paragraph was omitted entirely from AM and subsequently UP and PC:* As magistrates may lawfully call a synod of ministers and other fit persons to consult and advise with about matters of religion; so if magistrates be open enemies to the Church, the ministers of Christ, of themselves by virtue of their office, or they, with other fit persons, upon delegation from their churches, may meet together in such assemblies 1647; The ministers of Christ, of themselves, and by virtue of their office; or they with other fit persons, upon delegation from their churches, have the exclusive right to appoint, adjourn, or dissolve such Synods and Councils; though, in extraordinary cases, it may be proper for magistrates to desire the calling of a Synod of ministers and other fit persons to consult and advise with about matters of religion; and in such cases, it is the duty of churches to comply with their desire ARP

*Then the original 1647 sections3-5 were renumbered 2-4.*


(32.title) State of Man] AM, UP, PC; State of Men 1647, ARP

(32.2) and punished] AM, 1647, UP, PC; and be punished ARP


*In 1903 the following was inserted between Chapter 33 and new Chapter 34 in UP; it was subsequently dropped:*
PREAMBLE TO NEW CHAPTERS

Whereas, it is desirable to express more fully the doctrine of the Church concerning the Holy Spirit, missions, and the love of God for all men, the following chapters are added to the Confession of Faith.